Gardening
For Beginners

Gardening For Beginners

David Carr

WARD LOCK

ACKNOWLEDGEMENTS

The publishers are grateful to the following magazine and agencies for granting permission to reproduce the following colour photographs: *Amateur Gardening* magazine (pp. 2, 15, 50, 55, 62, 70, 75 and 91); Pat Brindley (pp. 11, 30, 59, 63 and 93); and Harry Smith Horticultural Photographic Collection (p. 87).

All the line drawings are by Nils Solberg.

First published in Great Britain in 1991
by Ward Lock Limited, Villiers House,
41/47 Strand, London WC2N 5JE, England
A Cassell Imprint
© Ward Lock Ltd

Text filmset in Formby
by Chapterhouse
Printed and bound in Portugal
by Resopal

British Library Cataloguing in Publication Data
Carr, David *1930–*
    Gardening for beginners.
    1. Gardening
    I. Title   II. Series
    635

ISBN 0 7063 6981 5

Frontispiece
Stepping stones in grass provide all-weather access without the stiffness or formality of paving.

CONTENTS

Preface   6

1   Assessing the site   7
2   Making a start   18
3   Soil fertility and texture   29
4   Plant raising   41
5   Planting and supporting   52
6   Simple pruning and training   66
7   Lawns and lawn care   79
8   Problem solving   91
    Appendix: Reliable garden plants for outdoors   94
    Index   96

PREFACE

Many of the failures and disappointments in gardening are avoidable – provided jobs are carried out in a workmanlike way, basic guidelines are followed and attention to detail is not overlooked.

This book sets out to be a confidence booster and ready reference for the newcomer to the gardening scene. The need for various vital jobs are pinpointed, and their correct implementation outlined in a proficient, safe and economic manner. In many instances this is with the aid of detailed, informative line drawings.

The techniques described are practical, well tried and proven. Once they are mastered, it is then quite feasible to expect to go on and make variations to suit individual circumstances. And this is what gardening is all about – nothing is ever totally 'rigid'. Compromises are the norm once experience is gained. Jobs considered to be beyond the scope of the inexperienced are indicated with comments.

Although intended primarily for the beginner, this book also has much to offer more experienced gardeners – even if only in the role of memory jogger.

Throughout the following pages, due regard is given to the principles and practices of healthy, environmentally friendly gardening.

The book is arranged systematically into eight chapters which cover the broad spectrum of operations in an average, newly acquired garden. Technical terminology is minimal, but where it is unavoidable an explanation is given at the relevant point. The text is written in a direct, easy-to-grasp style, with a comprehensive, sound approach. Illustrations and photographs clarify and supplement from start to finish.

This is a techniques book of gardening operations, and not a plant guide. However, in the appendix there are listed popular, reliable, easily grown and readily obtainable gardenworthy trees, shrubs, hedging plants, slow-growing conifers, climbers and wall shrubs, herbaceous and rock plants, as well as outdoor bulbs.

D. C.

CHAPTER 1

ASSESSING THE SITE

Although full of high hopes, the total newcomer, taking on his or her first garden, may feel a little insecure and lacking in confidence. Here before you lies your first ever plot of land. And for someone with no experience of outdoor plants or garden layout – where do you begin? What will you need in the way of tools? How will you know how to care for your plants if you cannot even identify them? What about fertilizers? If you have never had reason to lift a spade before, the list of possible questions is endless. Don't panic, the situation is not as daunting as it may seem. Throughout the following pages you will find advice to see you safely through most eventualities, and to help you avoid making the more common early and costly mistakes.

No matter whether you are taking on a new or an established plot, generally speaking your aims will be the same. And these are to get your garden into some sort of workable order as soon as possible. Don't be pressurized unduly by those around you. But do respect and don't ignore local knowledge – it can be invaluable.

TAKING OVER A NEW GARDEN

These days the ground is usually left in a reasonable state after building operations. But it is certainly not unknown – although rare – to find little more than builders' rubble outside your back door! Fortunately paths made and lawns laid is the normal state of affairs. And the owner is faced with the stark look of a brand new garden with its virgin grass and empty beds and borders. These need to be systematically prepared for planting – adopting the guidelines in succeeding chapters. Bear in mind there may be many hours of preparatory work before planting can begin. One of the main points to watch is that there is sufficient depth of topsoil for deeper rooting trees and shrubs – see p. 52. Frequently, there is only a token demarcation at the boundaries, so walling and fencing may also need some thought.

TAKING OVER AN EXISTING GARDEN

This may be the pride and joy of its previous owner, bursting with life in every corner and flower bed – or something a little more mundane. Either way, it is usually a matter of upgrading or making only minor adjustments in layout to suit the lifestyle of the new owner. Perhaps the best advice for any new gardener is 'Don't rush'. This is work which can be undertaken over a period of time. There is obviously less urgency than with empty beds. An established garden left to tick over for a while will continue to thrive at Nature's own pace. Take time to consider your needs. Perhaps the lawn needs extending – or a flower bed or two grassing over to reduce the workload? Conversely, enlarging the flower beds out into the lawn area may be an improvement? Most of you will want to replace the odd shrub or two with personal favourites. While running repairs will need to be made to fences and the like. Don't grub out shrubs if their identity is not known. Give them twelve months to see them through all seasons. Only then decide their true worth.

THE ESSENTIAL STARTING TOOLS

Spade – digging or border
Fork – digging or border
Rake – solid tine
Rake – spring tine
Dutch hoe
Pruners or secateurs
Pruning saw

Garden shears
Hand fork
Trowel
Watering can with rose attachment
Lawn mower
Hand sprayer or mister.

Over the following pages, other tools will be mentioned for specific tasks such as propagation and pruning. However, the above should see you through any immediate priorities. But buy tools as needed – not all will be required in all situations.

WHERE TO BEGIN – IMMEDIATE PRIORITIES

Carrying out alterations and improvements takes time and can involve considerable expense. So the most practical approach is to isolate any immediate problems, which obviously cannot wait, and deal with these first.

CHECKING FOR SAFETY

A garden, especially if neglected, can be a hazardous place for the unwary. But a brief inspection should soon reveal most of the pressing problems.

Look at footpaths, drives and other hard-surfaced areas, checking for sinkage and uneven surfaces liable to trip. Pay particular attention to steps and handrails, together with manhole and drain covers. If broken or missing, these obviously present real hazards.

Next, turn your attention to vertical structures like walling and fencing, including retaining walls and gateposts, and check that they are sound and not showing signs of movement. Make hedges and fences a high priority. With the risk of stating the obvious, they need to be made pet and toddler proof if children and pets are likely to frequent the garden. Granted this is not always within the control of the householder, as indeed is the case where restrictions are imposed by open plan housing schemes.

Water in whatever form – be it pool or stream – will attract children, and needs to be made safe. Proprietary grills for pools are one satisfactory solution, and they are quite inconspicuous once plants have grown through. If water features are to be retained, they must be accepted as a calculated risk to children.

Trees too should not escape scrutiny, especially if they are large and close to buildings, power or telephone lines. Danger signals of impending tree troubles include dead or dying branches and split trunks; leaning or undue swaying in high winds; movement at soil level – a gap between tree trunk and soil often spells instability. Any of these signs should be investigated promptly by a tree expert.

Be wary of any unfamiliar plants which carry berries – especially where these are brightly coloured and in an area where children play. On cultivated as well as wild plants, the berries may be poisonous; for example the red berries of yew, daphne, arum and nightshade can all cause a severe stomach upset if consumed by children.

CHECKING FOR NUISANCE

In descending order of priority, spotting and dealing with nuisance is next in ranking to safety. Often these two factors, safety and nuisance, are very closely intertwined. The main objective in the short term is to identify, and where practical eliminate, minor irritations until long term improvements can be carried out.

Overgrown hedges and shrubs which overhang footpaths and neighbours' gardens are not only a nuisance but are a potential safety hazard. This applies in particular to spiny/thorny plants which can injure eyes, tear clothing and scratch hands and face – and the family car. Pruning back is an immediate job.

Lawns which are broken up with numerous flower beds take longer to mow and there are more edges to cut. Many view them as a nuisance, resulting in extra work. Should some of these be levelled out and infilled? A wrongly sited tree, shrub or flower border may make it difficult to get in and out of the driveway with a car. Is grubbing out called for?

CHECKING FOR USAGE

Most householders view their garden as an extension of the home, with distinct areas designated for special purposes.

By convention, the front garden of many a house is the shop window of display and the reception area. Are paths and driveways adequate? Is future widening called for?

The majority of gardens have a patio of one sort or another, and with little effort most can quickly be transformed into an outdoor living room used for leisure, entertaining, eating and drinking. Where patios are to be extended, and where there is any choice in the matter, aim to build out on the warmest, sunniest, most sheltered and secluded side of the house. A quick calculation of the likely amount of patio space required is to allow a minimum of 2 sq m (yd) per person at any one time.

Have adequate utility areas been earmarked for refuse bins, fuel stores, garden waste, clothes drying and car washing? Or do any of these areas need extending or relocating? In the long term these important but less salubrious essentials are best screened from view, to render them as inconspicuous as possible. Similar considerations apply to space allowed for caravans, boats and any other accessories of outdoor pursuits.

Activity and/or play areas are a 'must' in the majority of gardens, perhaps for children or to serve as an overspill from the patio. This is where a hardwearing rear lawn comes into its own. It also provides an excellent setting for other garden features such as an ornamental pool, a rock garden, flower beds and borders, or statuary. Does the lawn need extending?

Finally, there is the vexed question of fruit and vegetable growing to consider. There are not the financial savings to be made of a few years ago, but what price to put on fresh produce – organically grown if preferred? Or indeed how to evaluate such a stimulating hobby? For success, fruit and vegetable areas need to be in sun for much of the day, and are also best screened from view. The enthusiast may want to make provision for a greenhouse or garden frame – they both need a sunny, sheltered spot, for to erect a greenhouse in shade is to restrict the number of crops which can be grown.

WORKING PLANS

Before allowing any contractor to embark on work, insist that a reasonably accurate working plan is prepared. It is folly to proceed without the when major improvements are being tackled. Such a plan has a two-way benefit: it forms a basis on which the contractor can price the job and execute the work; and from the householders' point of view, an essential price tag is agreed before work begins. It is also possible to visualize what the completed job will look like.

The easiest way for the DIY newcomer to tackle minor improvements is to go out into the garden with a few split canes to use as markers. Peg out any proposed extensions, reductions or relocations of hard-surfaced areas, lawns and flower beds and borders. Mark the positions of any trees, statuary, rock gardens and pools envisaged as focal points. With pegs in place, it soon becomes obvious if ideas are workable. If things look promising, make jottings and take a few measurements to use as memory joggers as the weeks go by. There are few new recruits to the gardening scene with the knowledge and the inclination to follow the oft quoted advice of 'measure the garden accurately and make a scaled plan on graph paper!'

A 'GOOD' GARDEN

One person's idea of what makes a good garden will differ from another's. And what is the best treatment for any specific garden must take into account its function and appearance. The climate, the soil and the needs of plants must also be considered if disappointments are to be avoided. Having said that, there are a few general basic guidelines which can usefully be borne in mind and are applicable to almost any garden:-

Simplicity of design and layout makes for ease of maintenance, with a consequent saving of time, effort and expense.

The design, layout and planting schemes should be practical and meet your own needs and lifestyle. What suits a neighbour may be totally inappropriate.

Planting needs to be in size, scale and proportion to the house and to the site. When it comes to the look of the garden, the desirability of an acceptable appearance throughout the year is the common factor. Otherwise the scope is

Conceal eyesores by the careful positioning of plants as here.

enormous and largely a matter of taste. Some prefer to have subdued colour and interest year round. Others opt for spasmodic bursts of brilliance at particular times of the year.

COMPLEMENTARY FEATURES OF A GOOD GARDEN

Paths and paved surfaces Grass is out of the question where heavy wear is likely and year round usage vital in all weathers, for example walkways from the house, to garage, patio, greenhouse or garden shed. In all these circumstances grass soon turns to a quagmire and hard surfaces are called for. When it comes to the choice of hard surfacing, don't choose in isolation – be mindful of the wide range of construction materials available. And when adding to existing hard-surfaced areas, always stick to the same type and colour of product as the original, to avoid ending up with a hotch-potch effect. Generally speaking, look to a low maintenance, hardwearing, easy to clean surface.

Concrete, tarmac and brick all look right in the company of brick buildings, but all need to be laid in a workmanlike manner. As does simulated stone, which suits stone-faced dwellings and walls. But here price tends to be a limiting factor. Concrete will provide an acceptable, basic, functional, inexpensive surface which will eventually mellow into almost any setting.

Gravel for paths and driveways can prove to be something of a problem. And gravel must never be viewed as an inexpensive option, for it most certainly is not when properly laid. Initially, it should be laid on a firm, deep, hardcore base; but even so, gravel paths and drives eventually become weedy. They need regular attention and they need topping up. Inevitably, too, gravel sooner or later finds its way onto the lawn to damage mower blades.

Crazy paving is another controversial subject, and it is not for the inexperienced to lay. It must be laid on a concrete base if uneven settlement and breaking up is to be avoided.

Paving slabs of one sort or another form a good serviceable surface, provided they are bedded onto a 5 cm (2 in) layer of level, well firmed sand. Paving slabs offer a good starting point for newcomers to try their hand at path and patio construction. Lay each slab onto five dabs of ready-mix concrete – a dab at each corner and one centrally is usually sufficient to prevent any side movement on the slabs. But even with paving slabs, time spent consulting a construction manual is time well spent – before making a start. Alternatively, get on-the-spot advice from a local builder.

Stepping stones (paving slabs set in grass). These make a useful access through the garden, without resorting to the rigid lines of a continuous path; and again, provided they are bedded on sand and dropped onto five dabs of concrete, they are quite steady and serviceable. But don't use slabs smaller than about 30 × 45 cm (12 × 18 in) or you risk some see-saw movement. Also, see that they are set 12 mm (½ in) below the surrounding lawn level, so as not to catch the mower blades.

Walls The present day tendency is to keep walling to a minimum – to reserve it perhaps for building retaining walls for terracing, constructing raised beds, or for building features like barbecues – and to turn instead to hedges and fences for barriers, screens, divisions and shelter.

Wall building, for whatever purpose, is not something to be undertaken lightly. The initial cost is high, and the beginner is well advised to leave the job to those with knowledge of the subject, as mistakes can prove costly – especially when it comes to retaining walls. These need adequate weep holes, and they need to be strengthened within precise limits if they are to withstand the considerable weight and force of soil and water from behind. The inexperienced could try their hand at low walling, such as around raised beds. But as with path laying, do consult a construction manual first.

From the gardener's point of view, the wind turbulence behind a solid wall makes life very difficult for plants, particularly in exposed gardens. The problem arises as the wind whistles over the top of the wall and then drops down behind with a swirling action. This is a problem which can be overcome, although at considerable cost. Use landscape/pierced walling slabs in preference to solid bricks or blocks, as they allow the wind to filter through and, in so doing, slow its speed and reduce its force.

The somewhat harsh appearance of walling can soon be softened with climbers and wall plants.

Fences come in many forms and have a major contribution to make in most gardens. In fact, it is probably true to say that fencing and hedging – individually or collectively – do more than any other feature to improve the environment within the garden. They create shelter and privacy for the benefit of both people and plants.

Use fences:

a) to provide instant results.

b) where space is limited. Fences take up relatively little space when compared to a hedge.

c) to camouflage and screen utility areas from view. Trellis, supported on posts, is useful for this sort of work, as it is for any partition or screen within the garden.

d) to provide a physical barrier. Boundary, close-boarded fences of about 1.8 m (6 ft) in height combine strength and durability with shelter. In exposed gardens, wind turbulence can be minimized by erecting 1.5 m (5 ft) high close-boarded fencing and then topping it with 30 cm (12 in) of open trellis.

e) to protect young hedging plants until they become established. Use something like wattle for the purpose; or, alternatively, picket-type fencing makes for a more upmarket finish. Traditionally timber vertical laths are attached to cross rails. The plastic version of today is equally effective and does not need painting.

f) to minimize the harmful effects of early morning sun after overnight frost. It is the over-rapid thaw which causes the damage to plants in these situations, and strategically placed fencing will provide shade and ensure a slow thaw. Trellis is useful to shade a choice bush or plant.

Maintenance of fencing All timber fencing and fencing posts need painting with preservative every couple of years or so. Where they are in close proximity to plants, use a safe horticultural preservative and not creosote which gives off damaging fumes on a hot summer's day.

Fencing posts Most fences are only as good as their supporting posts. And when erecting any fence, bear in mind that one quarter to one third of the total length of the post should be below ground if wind firmness is to be guaranteed. A 90 cm (3 ft) high fence needs 1.35 m (4½ ft) long posts. The portion below ground should be treated with preservative before burying.

The traditional method of erecting fence posts is to dig out a hole to the required depth and then set the post in the hole and concrete around. The modern way is to use proprietary metal sockets, although these again need to be pre-set in concrete for stability. Erect the posts as the makers recommend, but always allow at least three days for the concrete to set before bolting the post into the socket. Failure to observe this point can result in the bolts breaking up the concrete.

Hedging is highly effective for screening and for providing shelter from wind. With hedging there is little of the damaging air turbulence associated with solid walls and screening.

When considering the whole question of shelter, there is one useful calculation to keep in mind. On a level site, a hedge planted across the direction of the prevailing wind will normally provide effective shelter, on the leeward side, to a distance equal to four times its height. For maximum protection, the ends of any hedge should have a return, so that damaging wind doesn't swirl around the ends. When planning any layout, allow a minimum 1 m (yd) wide strip to accommodate a hedge comfortably.

Planted areas Success in any garden depends very much on having healthy plants that grow and flourish and are happy in their surroundings. One of the best ways to ensure that any new purchase will grow well is to match its needs, as nearly as possible, to the prevailing conditions of its allocated space – with particular reference to aspect, soil and shelter. It is generally cheaper, easier and a great deal more satisfactory to choose plants suited to existing conditions within the garden, than to try to modify the prevailing conditions of the garden to suit the plants.

Climate Is the garden situated in a mild, average or cold climate area, with very low winter temperatures?

Cut the maintenance of fussy, overplanted gardens, by grassing over the odd flower bed.

Aspect and shelter Note which parts of the garden receive midday and/or afternoon sun, and are sheltered from cold winds. These are the warmest, most favoured sites, well suited to sun-loving plants. Planting against a sheltered, sunny, warm wall is the most favoured site of all. Likewise, note those areas which are shaded and sunless, or receive only early morning sun. Note those areas which are cold and exposed to strong and chilling winds.

In short, the main things to establish – apart from climate – are which parts of the garden are sunny, which are shaded; and which are sheltered or exposed.

About the soil Whole books have been written on the subject! However, the main points the new gardener needs to be concerned with are soil depth, soil texture, soil acidity and soil nutrient levels – plus soil management.

Topsoil Check the depth of good topsoil by digging down and leaving a vertical profile exposed to view. The darker, fertile layer extending from the surface downwards gives the clue. How soon does it change to a paler, less fertile subsoil?

Soil acidity Aim to discover if the soil is acid or alkaline or somewhere between the two extremes. Many plants, such as rhododendrons and camellias, are likely to be unhealthy unless grown in acid soil. Others, like the cabbage family, are unhealthy and disease prone unless grown in alkaline, well limed soils.

Soil acidity can easily be checked at home using a 'soil test kit'. These kits are simple to use if you follow the maker's instructions. Briefly, soil samples are taken from various parts of the garden and, after removing stones, weeds and the like, are mixed thoroughly together. A small quantity of this mixture is then shaken up with a chemical and the resulting colour is compared with a colour chart. The degree of acidity or alkalinity is usually expressed as soil pH, where 7 is neutral, below 7 is acid and above is alkaline. The vast majority of garden plants grow happily in average soil with a pH of between 5.5 and 7.5; problems begin when the degree of acidity falls outside this range.

Soil texture too is very important. Sandy, gritty soils are easy to dig and work; they are normally free draining; and they warm up quickly in spring. However, on the debit side, they dry out quickly in summer, and hold little in the way of nutrient reserves. Heavy clay soils are difficult to work, so timing is all important. They must not be worked when they are over wet or over dry, or they will be even more difficult to cope with. These soils become iron hard and crack badly when dry. They are sticky and greasy to the touch when wet. In spring these are cold soils, and they warm up only slowly. Water is slow to drain away after heavy or prolonged rain.

Soil management In practice the treatment of all soils is basically the same: generous manuring and mulching are the keys to success, and provided generous amounts of manure are applied, even the heaviest soil will be improved in time.

CHOOSING PLANTS TO SUIT THE GARDEN

Climate Any good local garden centre will advise on which plants are hardy enough to survive in the district.

Sun and shade Many popularly grown plants can adapt to both sun and shade. The label, or a good catalogue, should indicate which plants must have sun and which must have shade.

Soil acidity Again, labels and catalogues should indicate any plant which must have acid soil or which must have alkaline. The pH of acid soils can be raised quite easily, and the soil made more alkaline, by liming. Lime-loving plants can then be grown. However, the same is not true of alkaline soils, where it is much more difficult to lower the pH and increase acidity. Where the soil is very alkaline, there is little alternative but to stick to lime-tolerant plants.

GUIDELINES ON SITING PLANTS

In gardening there are exceptions to most rules – but even so it can be helpful to point out a few basic points:

Sun lovers For sunny situations, select flowering trees, shrubs, herbaceous border perennials, bulbs and short-stay bedding plants. Grey-leaved plants, those with small or needle-like leathery thick or succulent leaves, and those with blue, gold, silver and red self or variegated foliage, as a rule also prefer to be in sun. Most aquatic plants need sun; as do the majority of herbs, vegetables and fruits.

Shade tolerance Shade-loving plants, and those able to adapt to shade, are mainly foliage plants with green or dark green, often large, thin leaves. Many evergreens come into this category. Shade-tolerant plants also benefit more from shelter than many of the sun lovers.

Wind tolerance In cold exposed or windswept sites, deciduous trees and shrubs, along with evergreen conifers with leathery, needle-like leaves, are better able to flourish than broad-leaved evergreens. Until shelter is provided, stick to low growing, ground hugging plants.

Town gardens In town gardens, especially where there is soot and grime to contend with, it is advisable to opt for shiny-leaved evergreens which can be hosed down from time to time. Avoid hairy-leaved evergreens, and conifers such as pine, spruce and fir; they all collect grime and tend to suffer from ill health when subjected to these adverse conditions. Most deciduous trees and shrubs are useful in towns, as they drop their leaves along with grime each autumn, and then start afresh again each spring. Similarly, herbaceous perennials which die down in autumn are a sound choice. And short-stay bedding plants which are cleared at the end of the season are also well suited to most town gardens.

HINTS ON USING PLANTS

Adopt the well tried rule of planting two evergreen plants to one deciduous. This avoids winter bareness in the garden.

To maximize on 'effects' in limited space, plant trees and shrubs which have more than one season of interest. Many have attractive fruits and foliage as well as flowers.

To reduce work, keep hedge heights to the minimum necessary. This avoids unnecessary ladder work and clipping at height.

To reduce work, keep down to acceptable levels the areas used for short-stay bedding plants and vegetables. These are amongst the most labour intensive of garden plants.

Plant labour-saving conifers and shrubs like aucuba, cotoneaster, euonymus and potentilla if time is limited. These require minimum attention.

Grassing over flower beds helps to cut down work for those who do not have the time, energy, or inclination to cope.

The newcomer to gardening would do well to study in some depth what is involved in rock, alpine and water gardening, before embarking on these projects. These are fascinating pursuits but there are pitfalls for the unwary.

CHAPTER 2

MAKING A START

Most newcomers to the gardening scene will either be faced with a garden to make from scratch, or take over one in a reasonable state of cultivation. Very neglected, derelict gardens are not the norm and should not be undertaken lightly. They are difficult for the beginner to tackle without on-the-spot advice. The problems are many and varied, not in the least of which is plant identification. It is not easy for the inexperienced to know which are weeds – what should be left and what disposed of. Then there is the question of pruning and cutting back neglected trees and shrubs; this always requires a lot more know-how and expertise than when dealing with routine pruning matters. Also, there are legal implications to think about – large trees may be protected by a tree preservation order, for instance. And the actual physical work involved is heavy by any standards; it is likely to be time consuming and it could be dangerous if tackled in the wrong way.

So, with these thoughts in mind, anyone landed with a neglected garden would be well advised to seek professional guidance. The pitfalls could then be pinpointed, a systematic way to tackle the job outlined, and in the long term a lot of money and time saved.

As a compromise, much of the work could be tackled DIY, with the heavy and skilled work contracted out. When it comes to equipment, a professional would be able to suggest suitable equipment to hire – perhaps with operator. Don't rush out and buy expensive equipment which is only going to be used once or maybe twice.

LEVELLING

Householders new to the gardening scene should only concern themselves with minor levelling.

Hollows in lawns should be levelled out, otherwise mowing is made difficult and standing water will cause puddling, slime, lichens and encourage weed encroachment (see page 88).

Hollows in flower beds should be evened out by taking soil from high spots and infilling the low. This is important because water standing around the necks of shrubs, or plants of any sort, can be the starting point of many root and stem rots.

Check the levels of flower beds butting up against the house. They must not lie above the level of the damp proof course, or you risk penetrating damp into the structure. Aim to lower levels so that two courses of brick, or the equivalent, are exposed below the damp proof course.

Level around beds and borders where they meet lawns and paths, ensuring a 5 cm (2 in) deep furrow. This takes care of surface run-off water and avoids the spread of soil onto paths and lawn. It also helps to prevent the nuisance of plant encroachment onto paths and lawn, as well as preventing lawn grasses from invading beds and borders. In terms of appearance it looks a great deal neater.

Level up after the removal of tree roots and the like. Where large holes are left, bottom out with stones and rubble, well consolidated to avoid sinkage at a later date. Top up with 30 cm (12 in) of good topsoil to just above the surrounding surface. This allows for settlement.

Level up loose paving stones and slabs by lifting and under-filling with sand and relaying them (see page 12). Where levels are critical, use a straight-edged piece of timber, pegs and spirit level. This way, slight variations in level are quickly identified.

Note Seek expert advice if there is any question of soil instability on steep slopes, especially if the construction of retaining walls is envisaged. Similarly, call in the experts if problems arise due to land sloping either down towards the house, or away from it.

DRAINAGE

Success in any garden depends on well drained soils. Water needs to percolate through the soil, to benefit plants in the process. Standing water can be serious, especially if it lodges around the necks of herbaceous plants, shrubs and trees, or causes waterlogging (complete soil saturation). Waterlogging leads to the drowning of plant roots, the build up of poisons in the soil and eventually, in extreme cases, the death of plants. Suspicious areas, where water stands around on the soil surface for any length of time after rain ceases, need investigation. Try to isolate the specific cause of the problem and then deal with it. A totally effective drainage system is likely to be achieved by a combination of construction work and soil cultivation.

ISOLATING THE PROBLEM

Starting with some of the more obvious causes of standing water:

Roof water Where water from any roof is allowed to fall unchecked onto borders underneath, flooding is inevitable, and that can result in waterlogging and root suffocation. The permanence of the flooding depends to a large extent on the nature of the soil – light sandy soils drain away the quickest. However, life on all soils is made virtually impossible for plants as soil is washed away to disturb and expose their surface roots to the elements.

Fit guttering and down spouts to all buildings, and preferably direct the rainwater into a water butt (see page 37). Where space is at a premium, and it is neither practical nor convenient to accommodate a water butt, direct the roof water into the nearest domestic drain.

Run-off water from paths and hard-surfaced areas Similarly water running off paths and large patio areas, onto nearby beds, can be a nuisance. Here French drains taken out alongside the hard-surfaced area can solve the problem.

Dig out a trench about 40 cm (16 in) deep and a minimum of 20 cm (8 in) wide. Make it wider where the problems are serious and the areas involved are large. Fill up the trench with small stones or broken rubble to within 5 cm (2 in) of the surface, and then level off with small chippings.

Another possibility to consider is the interception and diversion of excess water. Concrete gulleys built into paths and driveways can help. Construct these gulleys so that they channel the water to, and discharge it down, service drains.

Water run off from higher ground Whether the water is from a neighbour's garden – or your own garden – the treatment is much the same as when dealing with wetness alongside hard-surfaced areas. Take out a French drain to intercept the flow of water.

Sloping ground Surface water run off down sloping ground can cause waterlogging at the base, erosion and wash down, of soil and stones. This is a problem which can frequently be minimized by contour planting across the slope, provided the slope is not too steep. Ground cover shrubs like rose of sharon and periwinkle are ideal for the purpose (Fig. 1). Plant the shrubs closely to give dense ground cover quickly.

Fig. 1 Plant ground cover shrubs across slopes to minimize erosion and prevent waterlogging at the base.

Water standing around the base of a retaining wall needs prompt attention, or you risk destabilization of the wall. Seek the advice of a qualified surveyor.

Standing water on lawns See page 86 for spiking and topdressing. In extreme cases consider putting in a rubble-filled sump.

Blocked drains Check for blocked or broken drains and weeping water mains.

IMPROVING WATER PERCOLATION THROUGH THE SOIL

Where rain and irrigation water obviously have trouble draining through the soil, the cause of the problem can lie with the topsoil, the subsoil, or both (see page 15). Or it may be due to 'panning' somewhere in the top 60 cm (2 ft) (see below).

Where the topsoil is seen to be below par, set about improving fertility and texture by forking and working in copious amounts of garden compost and peat, together with coarse sand where the ground is inclined to be heavy. Repeat this treatment annually and it might be all that is necessary. On vacant land in these instances, deep double digging is sound policy.

If, on the other hand, the topsoil seems fertile and plenty of compost, peat or other organic matter has been forked in at regular intervals – with mulching as routine practice (see page 32) – and water *still* stands, then the fault probably lies in the subsoil. Where water cannot escape to lower levels down through the subsoil, it has no alternative but to accumulate after heavy downpours. During prolonged wet weather, the water backs up, reaching ever nearer the soil surface.

Where the subsoil is suspect, first check for 'pans' – impervious layers of soil through which plant roots and drainage water have difficulty in penetrating. Often pans are simply due to over-compaction of the soil, but they are sometimes more serious and due to chemical reactions in the soil. Either way, break them up by digging deeply and then work in copious amounts of organic matter to keep the soil 'open' in the future and prevent a recurrence of the problem.

If there is no suggestion of panning, then the situation calls for more drastic measures. The installation of one or more rubble-filled sumps provides one practical solution. These sumps are relatively easy and simple to construct, but it is really a fine weather job.

Construction of a rubble sump Selecting a low spot, near the problem area, dig out a 90 cm (3 ft) square hole of similar depth. First check that there is no danger of interference with mains services, electric cables, gas pipes and drains. Keep the good topsoil to one side when digging. Infill the hole with clean builders' rubble, to within 30 cm (12 in) of the top, firming to consolidate after each 10 cm (4 in) layer of rubble has been added. Failure to do this is to risk future subsidence. Top the rubble with a generous 5 cm (2 in) layer of fine gravel. This is to prevent any undue wash through of soil in the years to come. Level off with good topsoil, to just above the surrounding soil surface, so allowing for settlement. A sump of this size should drain an area of about 20 sq m (25 sq yds) on average soil, and slightly less on heavy land.

Note These days there should not be any serious drainage problems when taking over a house on a new development. Drainage should have been attended to as part of the ground works. The most likely problem is over-compaction of the subsoil due to heavy vehicle traffic.

CULTIVATIONS

Tools for soil cultivation

Buy hand tools to suit the operator and the main job in hand. Don't attempt to select a whole range of likely tools until your needs are properly assessed.

Barrow	Hoes
Spade	Cultivator
Fork	Solid tine rake

Why cultivate? It is an established fact that timely soil cultivations, aimed at creating and maintaining a good, fertile, weed-free soil, are vital to healthy plant life. Dig and prepare the ground thoroughly before planting, working in plenty of organic matter. Thereafter work the surface soil at regular intervals to keep it well loosened. Adequate supplies of food, air, warmth and moisture should then be ensured, all of which are needed directly by the plants themselves and by a thriving population of soil bacteria as well. The bacteria work away in the soil; amongst other things, they produce nutrients in a form plants can readily absorb through the root hairs.

It is impossible to be too dogmatic when speaking of surface cultivations. For instance on the vegetable plot, in empty beds and borders and amongst annual bedding plants, shallow surface cultivations follow on after deeper digging. However, in established borders only the top few inches are cultivated, and this is ideally prior to mulching.

DIGGING

Although digging is one of the most basic of all garden operations, in an average, modern, well stocked garden there is only limited scope to dig. In practice, dig when breaking in a new garden in readiness for long term planting of beds and borders; when preparing to lay a lawn; when taking any new area into cultivation; annually in the vegetable garden.

Advantages of digging

a) Aerates the soil. This enables it to warm up more quickly in spring, and in turn this speeds up plant growth and the breakdown of organic matter.

b) Relieves any soil compaction and improves the percolation of rain and irrigation water.

c) Makes it easier for roots to penetrate down to lower levels. Deep-rooting plants are more able to withstand drought.

d) Creates the ideal opportunity to work in manures. Frequent digging without manuring is bad practice.

e) Enables annual weeds to be buried and the roots of difficult perennial kinds to be removed.

f) Exposes soil pests on the surface, to be eaten by birds.

When to dig Heavy clay soils are best dug in autumn or winter. Winter rains, winds, frosts and thaws then 'weather' the soil to break down the clods ready for spring planting. Never dig clay soil when it is wet and sticky; and on really heavy soils it is often better to 'dig' with a fork.

Light sandy soils don't have the same need for winter weathering and can be dug at almost any time of year. However, winter weed growth can be a problem on these soils, especially in mild areas. For this reason, spring digging on light soils often ensures a cleaner start.

When digging, the aim should always be to allow sufficient time for soils to settle naturally before carrying out final preparations for sowing or planting. Puffy soils make poor seed beds.

How to dig For normal purposes, digging to the depth of a spade will suffice. Subsequently, rely on taking out deep individual planting pockets for setting out deep-rooting trees, shrubs and hedging (see page 53). Similarly in the vegetable garden, take out trenches for deep rooting crops like runner beans (page 64).

Starting at one end of the plot, take out a trench the full length of the bed, the width and depth of a spade. On the matter of depth be guided by the depth of good topsoil: don't bring up the inferior subsoil so as to end up by burying the good topsoil. Having taken out the trench, stack the soil to one side (Fig.2). Spread manure or garden compost into the bottom of the trench. Mark out a second trench alongside the first, again making it the width of a spade. Dig out the soil, invert and throw it forward into the first trench. For efficient working, aim to keep the sides of the trench as near to the vertical as possible and the depth of a spade. Manure the second trench and then mark out a third. Continue in like fashion until the end of the bed is reached. Fill the last trench with the soil from the first.

When autumn digging, leave the clods as they fall. The rough surface exposes a greater area to winter weathering. Break down the soil much finer when

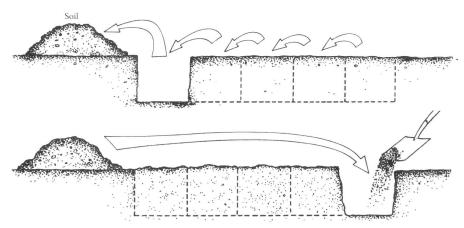

Soil

Fig. 2 Dig systematically, trench by trench. Invert the soil as it is thrown forward and infill the last trench with soil taken from the first.

digging in spring or summer.

If the bed is grass side up, the grass should be skimmed off, inverted in the trench in place of manure or compost and then chopped up. Over the turf sprinkle a handful of general fertilizer like Growmore per m (yd) run of trench. This assists in the decomposition of the turf.

Treat annual weeds like groundsel and chickweed in the same way as the grass: skim them off into the bottom of the trench. However, be thorough in the removal and disposal of the roots of difficult weeds like buttercup, dock, ground elder, couch grass and dandelion. These must not be buried.

Double digging is advisable on all neglected soils, and on compacted soils such as you might find on new building developments. During building operations soil can become over compacted. If this is then simply soiled over with topsoil, without first relieving the compaction, plant roots will find it virtually impossible to make their way down to lower depths.

Double digging is carried out in a similar manner to single digging, but trenches are taken out somewhat wider and the manure is forked into the bottom of the trench each time, down to the depth of the fork.

Note For those not used to digging, only attempt a little at a time.

FORKING

An alternative to digging with a spade Digging with a fork is often easier on stony, badly compacted and heavy soils. It can be quicker and it is acceptable to use a fork when preparing undug ground for planting in spring, provided the same procedure is followed as for digging.

As an alternative, or back up, to hoeing or using a cultivator By sliding the fork in at an angle of 45°, it is possible to use a border fork for the sort of shallow cultivations recommended as a preliminary to mulching, as it is for cultivating bare ground between growing plants during spring and summer. However, care is needed to avoid damage to plant roots by working too deeply, so prick lightly only.

To loosen and break down the topsoil in spring as a follow up to autumn digging, in preparation for planting.

For an end of season tidy up Lightly fork over permanently planted borders in autumn – working in any remaining organic mulches.

To break up the bottom of trenches and spread manure when digging

To break up the bottom and sides of planting pockets prior to forking in manure in preparation for planting.

To dig out weeds by their roots – especially useful when the soil is dry.

For compost making and trash handling

For spiking and aerating lawns

Note Use a narrow border fork between plants and growing crops. A standard digging fork is better for deep working and where space is not limited.

CULTIVATING

Soil is cultivated to break it down further after digging; to loosen compacted areas; and to clear it of weeds.

Cultivators usually have three or five prongs. In use a steady downward chopping and combing action is needed, drawing the curved tines towards the operator. Cultivators are easy to use and work well on all soils, but are excellent on stony and heavy soils where hoeing can be difficult.

In practice Cultivate in spring to break up the surface crust on land which was dug in autumn and has weathered down to a workable tilth. Only work the top 7.5 cm (3 in) or so of soil. This enables warm air and rainwater to penetrate, so coaxing soil bacteria into action.

Lightly cultivate permanently planted borders as an alternative to hoeing, and prior to feeding and mulching in spring.

Use a cultivator for inter-row cultivations between vegetable crops during spring and summer, primarily for weed control.

HOEING

Basically hoeing is a useful way to chop and cut the tops off seedling weeds; loosen compacted soil; and create a dust mulch to conserve moisture.

Several types of hoe are available, each one suited to a particular purpose.

The Dutch or push hoe is used with a skimming push and pull action, with the operator moving backwards. Its flat blade is used almost parallel with the ground (Fig. 3). Best reserved for easily worked soils.

Fig. 3 Use a Dutch/push hoe with a skimming push and pull action. Keep it going amongst vegetable plants during the growing season.

The draw hoe has a blade at right angles to the handle and is used with a chopping action to cut down weeds and loosen the soil. The operator moves forward over the loosened soil. This hoe is also used for taking out drills in readiness for sowing seeds, as well as for earthing up vegetables (Fig. 4). An effective tool for hard ground.

An onion hoe is invaluable for the rock garden and where plants are close together. It is a smaller, short handled version of the draw hoe and is used in a similar manner.

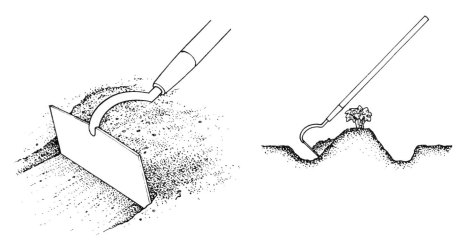

Fig. 4 Use a draw hoe for earthing up vegetables – drawing the loosened soil up around the stems.

In practice Lightly hoe permanently planted borders in spring, prior to feeding and mulching and as an alternative to cultivating.

Where mulching materials are in short supply, take a Dutch hoe and hoe bare soil in permanently planted borders regularly throughout summer. Also keep the hoe going amongst annual bedding plants and in the vegetable garden, constantly stirring the top inch or so of soil. Hoeing is particularly important on heavy soils prone to compaction, and after prolonged heavy rain when most soils suffer from a measure of surface panning.

Earthing up Use a draw hoe to earth up a variety of vegetable crops during the course of the season. Fork to loosen the soil, then draw the freshly loosened soil up into a mound around the plants in question. Take care not to damage roots or stems. Earthing up serves a number of purposes. Winter greens are supported. With leeks, the exclusion of light ensures the stems are suitably blanched. With potatoes, the developing tubers are prevented from turning green and they are given extra frost protection, while the risk of blight is also reduced.

RAKING
Soil work Metal rakes with solid teeth are used on soil. They are handled comb fashion – working the teeth back and forth (Fig. 5). This action serves to break down soil lumps, using the back of the rake to chop any which are stubborn. Use a rake to create a fine tilth, level out minor undulations, comb out stones and work in fertilizers. In short, a rake adds the final touches when preparing previously hoed or cultivated land ready for sowing or planting. Incidentally, the

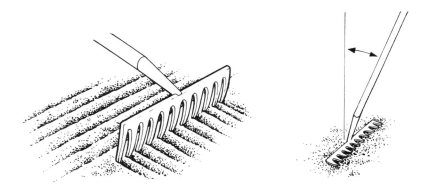

Fig. 5 Raking
Left. Use a rake comb fashion in the preliminary preparations of a seed bed.
Right. Final preparations – hold the handle near to the vertical to avoid working the soil too deeply.

back of a rake can be used as an alternative to a draw hoe when taking out drills in readiness for seed sowing.

Lawn work Spring tine wire rakes are best for use on lawns, for aeration, scarifying and leaf gathering (see page 85).

CHECKLIST

Preparing beds and borders for sowing and planting

1. Mark out positions of new beds.
2. Dig. Autumn digging is preferred on most soils, working in plenty of organic matter. Land needed for autumn planting is prepared during summer.
3. Lime during winter if needed.
4. In spring, break the soil down to a fine tilth. Either use a cultivator or fork lightly. Only work the ground when dry, and tread if puffy.
5. Apply fertilizers.
6. Rake down to the requisite state, ready for sowing or planting, and check surface levels. Create a shallow furrow around the edges of all beds and borders.
7. Mark out sowing and planting positions.
8. If there is a long interval between final preparations and sowing or planting, hoe off any weed growth and break up the crust.
9. Water dry ground and leave to soak overnight before planting.

· CHAPTER 3 ·

SOIL FERTILITY AND TEXTURE

Tools
(in addition to those items listed on page 8)

Bucket − 10 or 20l (2 or 4 gal)
Watering can with fine rose

Optional extras
Hosepipe with rose attachment
Spray nozzle for hose or hand sprayer

Plant growth, whether flowers, vegetables, fruits, shrubs or trees, depends almost as much on the soil as it does on the climate. While there is nothing much that can be done about the weather, there are many ways to bring any soil closer to the ideal − a good, crumbly, fertile loam.

MANURING AND SOIL CONDITIONERS

What is manuring? To manure a soil is to work in bulky organic materials; these are mainly composed of plant and animal remains.

Why manure? The main object of manuring is to improve soil texture. Although most bulky organic manures have some nutrient content, very often the supplementing of plant food is viewed as a bonus.

All soils, from cold, heavy clays at one extreme, to hot, light, dry sands at the other, are improved by manuring, and it is a practice which should be of high priority in any garden. Once manure is dug into the soil it is broken down by bacteria into humus, a brown crumbly material. On clay soils the humus improves the texture by coating the tiny clay particles. And so the soil becomes more crumbly, aeration is improved and surface 'caking and cracking' reduced. Surplus water is able to drain through more easily; and although the soil will still be moist, regular applications of manure will mean harmful waterlogging will be prevented. Conversely, on free draining sandy soils humus improves the moisture-holding capacity and plants are better able to withstand drought.

TYPES OF MANURE AND CONDITIONERS

Bulky organics Garden compost and leafmould make excellent manures (see Composting, page 38). Well rotted farmyard manure is good, but difficult to get hold of these days, and there is an ever increasing danger of the presence of harmful medicaments and antibiotics. Mushroom compost can be useful, but watch the lime content: it can be too high for lime-sensitive plants. Old growbags can be used as manure; and on occasions partly rotted straw, used as a mulch, is dug in as manure. If this practice is adopted, always dress the straw with general fertilizer, otherwise bacteria will temporarily rob the soil of nitrogen. They need a plentiful supply to sustain themselves as they struggle to break down raw materials like the straw. For peat, see Mulching on page 32.

Concentrated branded proprietary manures These products are gaining in popularity. They are pleasant, clean materials to handle and are sold in

Plastic sheeting provides a practical alternative where organic mulching materials like garden compost are scarce.

convenient packs. They are based on cow, poultry or horse manure, hops, seaweed, peat, domestic waste or shredded bark. Most are balanced to provide a very useful dual-purpose feed and soil conditioner. They seem expensive, but these are concentrated products and light dressings are the norm: applications are made in handfuls as opposed to barrowfuls in the case of bulky organics.

Minerals The likes of gypsum, dolomite, perlite, vermiculite, coarse sand and gravel when applied to heavy soils, will open them up to improve the texture, drainage and aeration.

Chemical soil conditioners These products are used to improve soil texture and come into their own where bulky organics are in short supply. Most are intended specifically for the short-term improvement of heavy clay soils. Many are based on gypsum or seaweed and temporarily break up large clods of clay particles. Long term improvement lies in the addition of bulky or concentrated organics and minerals.

APPLYING MANURES

The traditional way to apply bulky manure is to spread a layer into the bottom of the trench when digging. When dealing with concentrated proprietary manures it is often better to dig the soil, then fork the manure into the top 20 cm (8 in) or so. These methods are practical in the vegetable garden and on vacant ground. The easiest way to deal with permanently planted borders amongst herbaceous plants and shrubs, is to mulch in spring (see page 33), as worms will pull a surprising amount down into the soil, and any remainder can be lightly forked in during autumn. When planting trees and shrubs, dig manure into the bottom of planting pockets.

When to manure and how much Manure the soil every one or two years. If heavy clay soils are to be improved significantly, copious annual applications of bulky organics and minerals are called for. And if the moisture-holding capacity on sandy soils is to be raised to an acceptable level and then maintained, two or three bulky organic dressings will be needed during the growing season, given as a mulch. Think in terms of applying bulky organics at the rate of a bucketful per sq m (yd) at any one time on good soils. You will need at least twice as much on difficult soils. With other proprietary products, follow the maker's instructions. *Note* Don't manure immediately before growing root crops like carrots and parsnips, or risk forked inferior roots.

GREEN MANURING

On the vegetable plot and on other vacant land, green manuring can be beneficial. Quick maturing crops of mustard, or green manure mixtures, are sown; a few weeks later they are dug in, before they run to seed. Apply a general fertilizer to assist in the break down of the raw green manure (see under Straw, page 30).

MULCHING

Traditionally a mulch is a layer of bulky organic matter, such as well rotted garden compost or manure. It is spread on the surface of the soil around plants, mainly during spring.

Why mulch? The main purpose of mulching is to keep plant roots moist and cool during summer. This they are able to do firstly by reducing surface water evaporation during warm, dry weather. This increases moisture retention. In addition, during wet weather, bulky organics absorb surplus water and hold it in reserve for the future benefit of plants. Any undue wash out of soil nutrients is halted at the same time. Surface roots are physically protected from overheating under fierce summer sun, and generally kept much cooler. Clematis, wisteria, azalea, camellia, rhododendron and pieris all need a cool root run.

Mulches also suppress weed growth, so help to cut down on the work involved in and the damage done by hoeing off weeds. Many plants resent root disturbance during the growing season. Even light cultivations can be damaging to shallow-rooting plants like conifers, rhododendrons, heathers, lilies, dahlias, delphiniums and blackcurrants. Give these crops priority for any mulching materials going, and do away with summer cultivations.

Mulches prevent soil crusting and its adverse effect on plant growth. This is a problem common to unmulched soils as the season wears on, largely due to the action of rain and irrigation water beating down on the soil surface. Expect crusting to be particularly bad where plants are subjected to constant watering from cans and hoses during a dry season.

ORGANIC MULCHES
Well rotted garden composts and manures are the traditional mulches, providing some nutrients in the process. Never apply fresh manure as a mulch; allow it to rot first or risk scorching. Homemade leafmould also makes an excellent mulch. Mushroom compost can be useful too, but as some samples contain an appreciable amount of lime, play safe and reserve it for lime-tolerant plants. Present day proprietary bark mulches come in a variety of grades; be guided by your local garden centre. Most are very good; however, if your garden suffers from woodlice you are perhaps better opting for one of the other mulching materials.

Although peat makes a good mulch, it is expensive, adds nothing in the way of nutrients and there are 'green' issues at stake. Should the peat bogs continue to be depleted?

Be wary about using grass clippings for mulching. Compost them first to overcome the weed and slime problems; and never use clippings from lawns recently treated with weed killers.

PERFORATED MULCHING POLYTHENE

This is an ideal product for anyone short of organic mulches, as it is useful for retaining moisture and retarding weed growth. Look for two-coloured brands, white on one side and black on the reverse, and where it is imperative to avoid the overheating effect – as with shallow-rooting plants – use it white side uppermost. The chief problems with polythene are slugs and woodlice which thrive in the warm, dark conditions underneath and need regular baiting. Use as the makers direct. Covering the plastic over with chippings improves the appearance.

SPRING MULCHING

Spring is the best time to mulch around the garden. Get the mulch on before the soil dries out too much. Mulches must be applied to moist soils if they are to be effective. But don't mulch too early: let things warm up a bit first, otherwise soil temperatures will be depressed and growth delayed.

Hoe off the weeds, dress with fertilizer and water in – a small handful of general fertilizer like Growmore per sq m (yd) makes an average dressing. Only then apply the mulch. Don't allow the mulch to rest against plant stems – this is particularly important with soft-stemmed plants like herbaceous perennials. In permanently planted borders it is best to cover the whole area. But if this is not possible, then concentrate the mulch in deepish layers, not exceeding 5 cm (2 in), around individual plants (Fig. 6). If birds scatter the mulch, cover with netting pegged down at the edges. Try to keep the mulch replenished during the growing season and lightly fork in any remains during autumn. The mulch will then act as a soil conditioner. Bark mulches are the exception, as they are not dug in; they are left alone in autumn and the remains are pulled back in spring. This allows the soil to warm up naturally and quickly. The bark is then replaced and replenished as necessary.

Note When liquid feeding during summer, ease up the mulch to give better penetration.

AUTUMN MULCHING

This is usually reserved for marginally tender herbaceous plants and shrubs like agapanthus and alstroemeria, young camellias and magnolias. Mulch early to mid-autumn while the soil is still warm. Summer heat is then held and some frost protection given. It is advisable to remove autumn mulches temporarily in spring, otherwise the natural warming up of the soil tends to be delayed at this time.

Fig. 6 Mulching
Hoe the surface to loosen the soil, spread fertilizer, water it in and then apply the mulch
– keeping it away from plant stems.

FEEDING AND LIMING

Without a steady supply of fertilizers, starvation soon sets in – bringing weak
growth, poor roots and lack of fruit and flowers. While nitrogen, phosphate and
potassium are the chief foods for balanced growth, small amounts of iron,
magnesium, boron, calcium, and other nutrients too numerous to mention, are
also needed. However, these are normally present in sufficient amounts in any
reasonably fertile soil. In the main it is nitrogen, phosphate and potassium which
need supplementing. And one of the easiest ways to do this is to make regular
routine applications of a balanced, complete general feed.

PLANNED FEEDING
Aim to view plant feeding in two stages. Initially give pre-planting or pre-
sowing applications, and subsequently feed the growing plants.

Pre-sowing/planting dressings Rake dry applications of complete general
fertilizer (like National Growmore) into the surface when preparing the ground

for direct sowing, and similarly when preparing for setting out the likes of bedding, herbaceous and vegetable plants. A small handful per sq m (yd) makes an average dressing. For deeper rooting trees and shrubs, work the fertilizer into the bottom of the planting pockets and then infill around the roots with planting mixture or potting compost − both of which contain fertilizer.

Post-planting dressings These are strongly recommended around all long-stay plants each spring. Work the feed lightly into the surface and water in. Always feed prior to mulching (see page 32).

Dry feeds It is normal to use a general complete fertilizer for applications to long-stay plants, but on occasions a potting compost containing fertilizer is a better bet. This is true in the case of shallow-rooting shrubs like rhododendrons, azaleas and camellias. In these instances be sure to opt for a lime-free mixture. A topdressing of potting compost is also worthwhile in the rock garden, to replenish soil washed down by winter rains. And for long-term plants being grown in containers, topdress with potting compost in the years they are not repotted. In this case scrape off the top 1 cm (½ in) of old potting compost before applying the topdressing.

Liquid feeds give plants a quick, but short-lived boost. They are ideal as a back-up to dry spring feeds and are likely to be essential on light soils − and in high rainfall areas − where many plants can become starved before the end of the growing season. This is also true of container-grown plants and for these, too, liquid feeds are recommended. In the case of hungry fruiting or flowering crops, salads and greens, repeated, often weekly feeds are called for throughout the growing season. Select balanced high potash (potassium) feeds for all flowering and fruiting plants. Liquid feeds are easy to mix and use − follow the maker's instructions.

Applying fertilizers Avoid exceeding recommended application rates − the risk is root scorch.

Avoid leaving pockets of high concentrations of fertilizer, as even distribution is essential.

Never apply feed to wilted or dried out plants; water first to avoid root damage.

Never use stale fertilizers as they can be harmful.

LIME AND LIMING
Why lime? Lime has a big influence on soil fertility. In addition, the calcium supplied is an important plant food.

The most important effect of liming is to neutralize excessive soil acidity. An unduly acid soil restricts the work of beneficial bacteria and other soil life, and slows the breakdown of organic matter. Many plants find difficulty in taking up phosphate on very acid soils. Lime also has a direct beneficial effect on soil texture. Take heavy clay soils as an example. When limed, the tiny clay particles loosely unite to form larger crumbs, improving texture, drainage and aeration.

What to use Lime is normally applied in the form of ground limestone. Initially the amount to apply can be ascertained by soil testing with a DIY kit. These kits come complete with instructions and are simple to use. Thereafter, a handful per sq m (yd), one year in three, should suffice. Clay and peaty soils can be limed more generously than others, say every two years.

How to lime On vacant land, as on the unplanted vegetable plot, ideally scatter lime on the surface after digging in autumn or winter. But only lime a portion of the plot each year. Aim to rotate crops so that lime-loving members of the cabbage family are grown on the limed part in the first year, peas and beans in the second, and potatoes in the third, as the soil is reverting back to acid. In the case of fruits and permanently planted beds and borders, sprinkle lime around the plants in autumn and allow the rain to wash it in.

Guidelines for liming Lime if the soil is unduly acid.

Lime when preparing the ground for lime-loving crops, like members of the cabbage family.

Don't lime if the soil is already chalky or limy. Excessively limy soil prevents plants from taking up boron, iron, magnesium and other nutrients needed for healthy growth.

Don't lime when growing lime-hating plants like rhododendrons, azaleas, heathers and potatoes.

Don't apply lime at the same time as fertilizers and manures, or you risk a chemical reaction and loss of nutrients. Allow a gap of 10 days or so.

WATERING

Never a dry season passes without stringent water restrictions being brought into force. This is why it makes good sense to concentrate in the long term on improving soil texture and mulching generously. This is in an effort to conserve moisture, promote healthy growth and drought-resistant plants. The alternative is to rely on applying copious amounts of water during prolonged dry weather. Of course some crops and some plants are more drought-resistant than others. In the vegetable garden for instance, opt for 'bolt resistant' varieties wherever possible. To bolt is to run prematurely to seed — very often brought on by a setback of some sort like drying out.

COLLECTING WATER

As a buffer against restrictions, install a water butt — or two — to collect rainwater from your garage, shed, greenhouse or dwelling roof. Regardless of restrictions, a supply of rainwater is very useful, particularly if lime-hating plants are grown in hard water areas where the tap water contains lime.

ALWAYS WATER:

1. Container-grown stock before planting out.
2. The bottoms of seed drills before sowing in dry weather, using a can with fine rose.
3. The bed prior to setting out bedding plants in dry weather. Allow about 10 l per sq m (4 gal per sq yd) and apply through a fine rose.

ENSURE THE FOLLOWING ARE KEPT MOIST:

1. Container plants.
2. Seedlings.
3. Young growing plants in both the flower and the vegetable garden.
4. Anything newly transplanted.
5. Fruits, as the crops are swelling.
6. Shallow-rooting plants.

Note Never let plants wilt through lack of water — irreparable damage can be done.

APPLYING WATER

In small gardens, stick to a watering can or hose for general use, as they give a greater measure of control when compared to the automation of seep or trickle hoses.

Always water with a rose attachment fixed to your hose or watering can — never use them open-ended. The danger is that water is applied too quickly, causing damage to both plants and soil, and as plants are flattened and soil washed away from their roots, the ground becomes compacted. The need for slow water application is of particular significance on heavy soils. When subjected to a deluge of water, they are liable to puddling with the subsequent formation of a damaging surface crust.

Concentrate the water around the base of all newly set out plants i.e. practise ball watering until established (Fig. 7).

Water generously at each watering. Never water in dribbles. This is counter-productive since it encourages shallow rooting with the consequential inability to withstand future droughts.

Don't water plants in strong sun in case of leaf scorch; wait until the evening. In shaded areas, however, try to water early in the day, as this gives the foliage time to dry by nightfall and reduces the risk of fungal diseases.

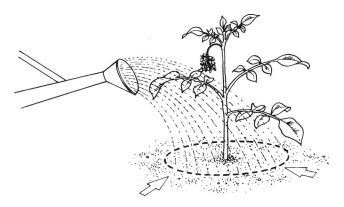

Fig. 7 Concentrate the water around the base of all newly set out plants.

During dry, warm or windy weather, spray over newly planted conifers and evergreens in the evenings – using clean water. Similarly spray over growing crops of beans and tomatoes to promote a good set of fruit. In the absence of a sprayer, a watering can with fine rose attachment will do an acceptable job.

MAKING GARDEN COMPOST

Although there are various ways to make garden compost, all have the same objectives in common, to create ideal conditions for beneficial bacteria to thrive. A warm, well aerated, free draining, non-acidic environment is needed. Success with compost depends on a healthy population of bacteria, which break down green vegetation into the sweet smelling, brown, crumbly, valuable manure known as garden compost.

COMPOSTING IN BINS

The easiest and tidiest way to make good compost in a small garden is to use a proprietary compost bin of some sort. Bins with slatted wooden sides are traditional, and when lidded they provide close to ideal conditions. Those with one side that is removable make for ease of access.

Plastic bins with perforated, insulated sides keep in warmth and regulate aeration; their tight-fitting lids reduce heat loss to a minimum and keep out rain, so eliminating the wash-out of valuable nutrients (Fig. 8). In small gardens it is often best to opt for the type of bin where green material is fed in at the top and rotted compost forked out at the bottom, as an ongoing process.

Another useful type of plastic bin has sloping unperforated sides. In use the bins are simply lifted off to expose the rotted compost. It is very important not to

Fertilizer

Vegetation waste

Coarse material

Lid

Fig. 8 Solid-sided compost bins are lifted off to expose the rotted compost. Eminently suitable for the serious compost maker and large gardens where it is usual to have two or three bins alongside each other.

over-consolidate in this type of bin, so read the maker's instructions carefully.

In large gardens, consider two or even three bins, with the idea that as one bin is being filled another is rotting down and a third being emptied.

A cheaper alternative to bins is to build up the compost in a free-standing heap. Provided the heap is kept covered with heavy duty plastic, well weighted down at the corners to exclude rain and keep in warmth, a free-standing heap is quite satisfactory. However, aim to make the heap at least 90 cm (3 ft) square to create sufficient warmth. The chief drawback to this method is that free-standing compost heaps always tend to look rather untidy in small gardens.

Making the compost Whether you are working with containers or free-standing heaps, unless a bin with a fixed perforated base is being used, begin by creating a well drained base. An 8 cm (3 in) layer of brushwood is best, but stones will suffice. Healthy vegetation waste is then built up, sandwich fashion, gradually throughout the season. Lay down layers of about 10 cm (4 in) at a time, alternating the green materials with a sprinkling of general fertilizer. The alternative is to use proprietary compost activator as the makers recommend.

The more varied the mix of waste materials the better. Aim for a balance of coarse waste and fine. Chop up coarse materials and mix with the likes of lawn clippings. Dry fibrous materials will not rot down satisfactorily on their own; and if too much soft, succulent waste is included, such as unrelieved grass clippings, the compost is likely to lack aeration and become a slimy, evil-smelling mass. A good sample of garden compost has a pleasantly earthy smell – and is brown and crumbly in texture.

What to include Lawn clippings, annual weeds, household vegetable trimmings, pea and bean haulm, soft deciduous hedge trimmings in moderation and deciduous leaves can all be added to the compost heap/bin. Never include weeds that are setting seeds; difficult perennial weeds like couch, buttercup, nettle, dock, ground elder, thistle and convolvulus; pest and disease infected plants; woody material like brussels sprout stalks; chemically treated weeds or lawn clippings; anything contaminated with creosote or other wood preservative; or cooked vegetable waste and anything greasy – they will only attract vermin.

Where large quantities of compost are envisaged – say, to improve difficult soils – rarely are sufficient quantities of compostable materials available in small gardens. Under these circumstances, it is well worth buying in straw (or similar) to make up bulk. But do first check on the possibility of chemical contamination in the form of weedkillers and the like, and give such products the go by. Perhaps spent hops may be available at a local brewery? They too are useful to make up bulk.

How long does it take? Compost can be ready to use within four months or less, but a lot depends on the season. Waste put down at the beginning of winter is going to take a lot longer to decompose than the same amount put down in spring. When emptying the bin/heap, use any incompletely rotted compost from the outside to start off the next heap.

MAKING LEAFMOULD

Deciduous leaves (not evergreen) can be included in the general compost bin, but because the addition of any quantity of leaves to the general bin tends to slow down rotting, many gardeners prefer to compost them separately into leafmould. Again, a compost bin is the tidiest way of dealing with leaves. But a cheaper alternative, where space permits, is to construct a compound of about 90 cm (3 ft) square and of a similar depth. Make it in an out-of-the-way spot. Attach chicken wire to four corner posts, line with perforated plastic, and keep covered between fillings. Moist leaves are built up in layers in the same way as when composting general vegetation.

CHAPTER 4

PLANT RAISING

Many newcomers to the gardening scene fight shy of propagating plants. This is a pity because it is not all that difficult. Indeed there is little to lose by 'having a go'.

Tools for plant raising
(additional to those cited on pp. 8, 22 & 29)

Pruners/secateurs	Propagator
Hand fork – short handled	Sieve or sugar sifter
Trowel	Knife – pocket or garden.

SEED SOWING OUTDOORS

WHEN TO SOW
Sowing time needs to be related to local conditions, the weather, the state of the soil and to the crop concerned. Some seeds are best sown in spring and others in late summer; but when it comes to the likes of salads and quick maturing vegetables, they are sown at regular intervals throughout the growing season to keep up a succession of produce.

SEEDS
Buy fresh seed of varieties known to do well locally. Check that they are suitable for the season and method of cropping. For instance, keep to outdoor varieties for growing in the open and never try to use indoor kinds.

Standard varieties are suitable for most purposes, as they give reliable average crops of reasonable quality. F_1 hybrids are generally more uniform and vigorous than standard varieties, but they cost more. Mid-way in cost and performance come the F_2 hybrids.

Untreated seeds are still the most widely used, but for ease of handling some gardeners turn to pelleted seeds which are coated with fertilizer and fungicide. Others push in 'sticks' – these seeds are sold in packets, rather like tear off matches.

Note If seed cannot be sown right away, keep it cool at about 5°C (40°F), in a shaded, dry spot protected from vermin. Don't open the packet until the last moment, to prevent moisture and disease organisms gaining entry. Immediately after sowing, protect any surplus seed by resealing the packet and returning it to cool, dry, shady conditions.

PRE-SOWING PREPARATIONS

Avoid sowing in shaded areas under the drips of trees; on ground which has carried a similar, or closely related, type of plant within the previous two years.

Take account of the season It is sowings made early and late in the season which present the greatest difficulties, so give these crops priority for favoured, sunny, sheltered spots. In spring, about a fortnight before the earliest sowings are envisaged, aim to cover the soil with cloches, to help it dry out and warm up. Then after sowing, protect the seeds with cloches. Where this is not feasible, delay sowings until things warm up a bit.

Soil preparations Once the time is right for sowing, and assuming the soil has been well prepared (see Chapters 2 and 3), you can set about final preparations. Break up any remaining hard clods with the back of a solid tine rake (alternatively, use a cultivator). Then firm the soil, if it is inclined to be puffy, by treading heel to toe. Never try to force the pace by working the soil when it is wet. Apply general fertilizer like Growmore at the rate of a small handful per sq m (yd). See page 35 for liming. Finally, using the rake comb fashion, work the seed bed down to a fine crumbly tilth, always working backwards to avoid walking on the raked area.

Seed treatment Most flower and vegetable seeds are sown without any special treatment. But follow the instructions on the seed packet as peas, for example, are best soaked.

SEED SOWING

Drill sowing

The 'V' drill is practical for sowing small and medium-sized seeds. It is extensively used, both when sowing to harvest or flower *in situ*, and when sowing in a nursery bed to raise young plants in readiness for transplanting. A shallow furrow is scratched out alongside a taut line, using a draw hoe or the back of a rake (Fig. 9). Relate furrow depth to size of seed; a good rule of thumb guide is to set untreated seed at a depth equal to three times its diameter, and make it twice in the case of pelleted seeds. If the soil is dry, water the bottom of the drill, using a can with rose, and allow the water to seep in before sowing. Pour small and medium-sized seeds into the palm of your hand and then, using forefinger and thumb, sow a pinch at a time, working systematically along the row. For those who prefer seed dispensers, there are various suitable models available.

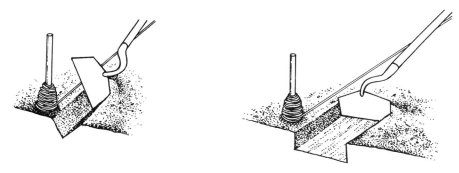

Fig. 9 Seed drills
Left. Use a draw hoe to take out a 'V' drill alongside a taut line in readiness to sow small to medium sized seeds.
Right. Taking out a flat–bottomed drill suitable for sowing large seeds like peas.

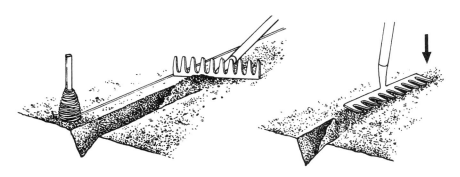

Fig. 10 Using the back of a rake to cover sown seeds
Left. Push the soil to backfill the drill.
Right. Lightly tamp to settle the soil.

Larger seeds and pelleted seeds are spaced out individually. After sowing, gently draw loose soil over the seeds with a rake. Then lightly tamp, using the back of the rake with the handle held vertically, to firm the soil (Fig. 10).

The flat-bottomed drill Flat-bottomed drills are useful for sowing large seeds like peas. Using a spade or draw hoe, take out a drill of about 5 cm (2 in) deep and 12.5 cm (5 in) wide. Seeds are scattered evenly and thinly over the base and then covered over, as for the 'V' drills.

Exceptional circumstances In cold wet districts on heavy soils it is best to draw up slight ridges of about 20–30 cm (8–12 in) in width and 10–12.5 cm (4–5 in) in height. Drills are then taken out along the top of the ridge and the surface water is able to drain away more freely. There are few vegetable crops which don't benefit from this treatment. Conversely, in dry areas on quick draining soils, take out drills in the bottom of shallow trenches, so trapping and making use of any surface run-off water.

Station sowing Large seeds like broad beans and pelleted seeds can be sown singly in rows, without taking out drills. Use a blunt-ended dibber to make each hole or 'station'. This is also a satisfactory way of sowing the likes of parsnips, sweet peas and marrows, but here two or three seeds are sown at each station and then the seedlings are later thinned to leave the strongest. The chief thing to watch with station sowing is that the seeds are not sown too deeply.

Surface sowing Some fine seeds are simply scattered on the surface of the soil and then barely covered with potting compost. Flower seeds like foxgloves and forget-me-nots are treated in this fashion. Fine mesh netting, laid over surface sown seeds and pegged down in place, helps to ensure more rapid germination and gives added protection against heavy rain and birds. Remove the netting as soon as the seeds germinate.

AFTER SOWING

Mark and label all sown seeds and the area they occupy. This is so the young seedlings can be more easily distinguished from weeds later on. Keep the seeds moist until there are signs of movement, watering daily if need be, although ease up on watering once the first true leaves develop (to encourage plants to make deeper roots and so be better able to withstand drought in the future). When seedlings reach about 3 cm (1 in) in height they are ready for thinning, to leave plants standing singly. Follow the instructions on the seed packet for spacings. See Chapter 8 for protection of newly sown seeds.

STEM CUTTINGS

Stem cuttings are one of the most practical and popular ways of raising plants. But the way these cuttings are taken and subsequently treated must be varied to suit the plant in question and be linked to the time of year and the state of the 'wood'. However, there is a degree of flexibility. Some cuttings will root readily when taken at both the soft and semi-hardwood stage – and others when taken at the semi-hardwood or hardwood.

Only ever take cuttings from plants which are vigorous and healthy. Some diseases are transmitted from one generation to the next, and cuttings taken from stunted or starved plants are usually reluctant to root and invariably prove to be a waste of time. Finally, only consider taking cuttings from plants worthy of duplication – bad as well as good features will be passed on.

SOFT AND SEMI-HARDWOOD CUTTINGS

General guidelines Take cuttings from shoots which are not carrying flowers or flower buds.

Take cuttings early in the day when they are most likely to be fully charged with water.

Use a sharp knife or secateurs to remove the cuttings from the plant, and a sharp razor blade for the final trimming.

To prevent cuttings wilting before they have been potted up, drop them into a plastic bag and seal.

Prepare small pots of proprietary cutting compost in advance. This is so that there is as little delay as possible between taking the cuttings and potting them.

Although not essential, proprietary rooting preparations can help to prevent rotting and speed up rooting. But do read the label and use the one intended for the particular type of cutting in hand.

Dip cuttings with milky sap into charcoal before potting.

Using the blunt end of a pencil to make small dibber holes before inserting three or four cuttings around the edges of small pots of cutting compost. Set them to no more than a third their length and take care not to bury the leaves to avoid any risk of rotting.

In the absence of a garden propagator, encase the entire pot of cuttings in an inflated clear, perforated plastic bag, held in place with an elastic band. This is to maintain high levels of humidity; in addition, spray the cuttings regularly with tepid water.

Cuttings root well on a warm indoor sill in good light, shaded from strong sun. But the bottom heat provided by a propagator or seed tray soil warmer will speed things up.

After rooting pot up the young plants. But before they can be planted outside they must be gradually acclimatized to outdoor conditions if they are not to suffer a setback and irreparable damage. This is often referred to as hardening off. Put the young plants outside for a few hours each day. And then gradually increase the amount of time they spend outdoors until eventually they can stay outside in safety overnight. Allow two or three weeks for hardening off.

Soft stem cuttings are taken from the tips of shoots which have not yet begun to harden. This is a useful way to increase plants with succulent stems, including perennial bedding plants such as geranium, busy lizzies, heliotrope and calceolarias; herbaceous border perennials; soft stemmed rock plants; as well as sub-shrubs.

This type of cutting is taken any time between early spring and summer. Select a firm young shoot and avoid those which are soft, thick and over sappy, along with any that are weak and spindly. Aim for a cutting of 2.5–7.5 cm (1–3 in) in length after trimming; it must include a minimum of two leaf joints.

Fig. 11 Taking softwood cuttings
Left. Removing a firm, young tip shoot from parent plant.
Centre. Trim just below a leaf joint and remove the lower pair of leaves.
Right. Insert prepared cuttings round the edges of small pots of cuttings compost.

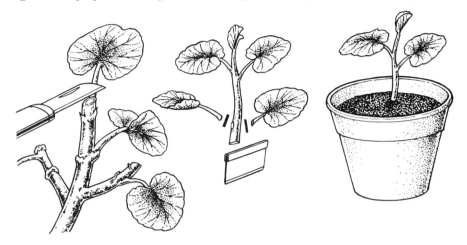

Trim the cutting cleanly and squarely, just below the bottom leaf joint (Fig. 11). Strip away the lower pair of leaves and insert in cutting compost.
Note Geraniums are an exception. They should be allowed to wilt slightly overnight before insertion in cutting compost.

Semi-hardwood cuttings can be taken from a whole range of shrubby plants – pretty well anything in the garden is worth a try. Take the cuttings in summer as soon as young growths have partially ripened and begun to harden. Select terminal shoots and cut well into the hardened wood. After trimming cuttings should be 10–15 cm (4–6 in) in length.
The standard method Basically treat as for the soft stem cuttings. However, one essential difference is that the soft tip should be cut out, just above the top pair of leaves.
Heel cuttings Pull a sideshoot downwards from a main stem so that a sliver of main stem remains attached to the base of the cutting. This is known as the 'heel'. Trim to neaten any straggly tails on the heel (Fig. 12). Cut out the soft tip. And then proceed as for the soft stem cuttings.

HARDWOOD CUTTINGS
Hardwood cuttings represent a reliable way to increase a whole range of hardy shrubs, including favourites like weigela, forsythia and escallonia – as well as fruits like currants and gooseberries.

Heated propagators provide the extra warmth needed to speed up the rooting of cuttings.

The best time to take hardwood cuttings is mid–autumn, just as the leaves fall with deciduous kinds. Not only is the wood ripe at this time, but the soil is still warm enough to give them a good start. They are usually rooted in a sheltered spot outdoors.

Select shoots from vigorous, sound stems which have just finished their first year's growth. They should be well ripened and firm. Cut the shoots out with

10–15 cm
(4–6 in)

Fig. 12 Taking semi–hardwood cuttings

Left. Pull a sideshoot downwards, so that a sliver of main stem comes away with it.
Right. Cut out the soft tip, remove the bottom pair of leaves and trim the 'heel' to neaten.

secateurs, near to the joint with the main stem (Fig. 13). Alternatively, take the cuttings with a 'heel' (see page 46). Either way, trim as for the semi-hardwood cuttings, ending up with a cutting of 20–30 cm (8–12 in) in length.

When dealing with cuttings from deciduous shrubs, remove any remaining leaves. With evergreens, trim to just below a leaf at the base and to just above a leaf at the top. And then remove the leaves from the lower half. When dealing with large-leaved evergreens, cut the leaves crosswise, cleanly in half. This helps rooting by reducing the loss of moisture and subsequent strain. Mexican orange, laurel and evergreen hydrangea all respond to this treatment. In a similar vein, spray evergreens with a proprietary anti-wilt preparation to cut down moisture loss and speed up rooting.

Prepare the bed for rooting prior to taking the cuttings. Select a sheltered spot, protected from north and east winds. It is important to prepare the soil thoroughly, working in plenty of sand if it is inclined to be heavy. Make a series of dibber holes about 15 cm (6 in) deep and about 10 cm (4 in) apart. Bottom them out with coarse sand. Insert a prepared cutting into each hole, firming the soil well around the cutting and ensuring its base makes close contact with the sand.

From here on, don't allow the cuttings to dry out at any time. Keep them weed free and stir the soil crust from time to time. Refirm the cuttings after frost or wind; the base must always be kept in close contact with the sandy soil.

Cuttings vary considerably in the time they take to root, but one or two years is the norm. Move them into their permanent positions when well rooted and growing away freely.

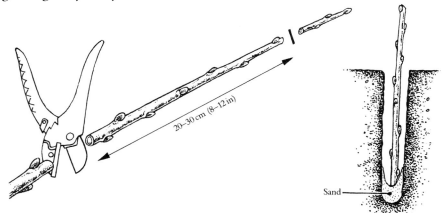

Fig. 13 Taking hardwood cuttings
Left. Select a firm, ripe shoot and cut off the soft tip.
Right. Root outdoors in a sheltered shaded spot. Bottom out dibber holes with sand, insert cuttings and firm back the soil so that the base of the cutting is kept in close contact with the sand.

DIVISION

Division is one of the easiest, most basic and cheapest methods of propagation. Large plant clumps are simply split up into several smaller ones – or in some instances small plantlets are detached from the sides. Newcomers to gardening will be dealing in the main with clump-forming herbaceous and rock perennials, and naturalized bulbs.

Note Only ever divide plants which are healthy.

After you have carried out a division, aim to move the new plants to a fresh part of the border, switching them round with different kinds of border plants. This is to prevent a build up of pests and diseases.

Most clump-forming perennials should be divided every three to five years as a matter of routine in a rejuvenation process, regardless of whether more plants are needed or not. Neglect in this respect leads to overcrowded, weak-stemmed plants with few and inferior flowers. Provided a reasonable standard of cultivation is maintained, and a few basic rules observed, healthy plants should remain in good condition indefinitely, when divided up at regular intervals.

DIVIDING CLUMP-FORMING HERBACEOUS BORDER AND ROCK PERENNIALS

Plants flowering in early spring are best dealt with in autumn. Otherwise the job can be tackled any time between mid-autumn and early spring, so long as plants are resting and the soil is neither frozen nor over wet.

Systematically working all round the clump, loosen with a garden fork, ease up and lift. Poke soil, small stones and weeds out from amongst the roots with a pointed stick. It is then very easy to pull young plants apart by hand. Just make sure each portion has some healthy roots and strong buds. Trim away any damaged roots and dead leaves before replanting the young, actively growing, outside portions of the clump. Always dispose of worn out pieces from the centre of the clump. And always work quickly so that the roots don't dry out. Older neglected plants are more difficult to deal with, as very often their roots are well entangled. Using a spade, chop them up into reasonably sized portions, then deal with them as above and they will be easier to cope with next time they are lifted.

The majority of popular border and rock perennials are treated in this manner.

DIVIDING OFF PLANTLETS

Strawberries are increased by removing plantlets. Keep up a succession of young plants by pegging down plantlets into small pots of potting compost in early summer. Don't pin down more than four plantlets from any one healthy plant. Each stem/runner may carry several plantlets: it is the one nearest the parent which is used (Fig. 14). Cut off the portion of stem beyond the pegged down plantlet, along with any other surplus runners. Once the young plants are growing freely, they are severed and planted up in fresh ground.

DIVIDING UP NATURALIZED BULBS AND CORMS

(those which are left in the ground to come up and flower year after year). Like herbaceous perennials, naturalized daffodils, narcissi, crocus and snowdrops

Divide flag iris into segments. Shorten each leaf–fan by half and replant promptly.

Fig. 14 With strawberries, the plantlet nearest the parent is pinned down into a small pot of potting compost. Cut off the remainder of the stem beyond this point.

need to be lifted and divided periodically, when they become overcrowded and flowering deteriorates.

In the case of daffodils, narcissi and crocus, gently fork up the clump after the foliage has died down. Separate the bulbs and corms and grade them for size. Put the largest to one side ready for planting in their flowering positions. The smaller ones need to be grown on for a few years, in an out-of-the-way spot, until they have made sufficient size to flower. Either replant the bulbs and corms immediately, giving the flowering-sized ones a bit of fresh ground and a bit more room, or alternatively dry them off and replant in autumn.

Snowdrops are different. Deal with them immediately they have finished flowering and are still carrying plenty of leaf. Split them up; they must be replanted without delay or suggestion of drying. Water in after planting.

SIMPLE PEG LAYERING OF HEATHERS

Heathers are readily increased by pegging down vigorous young growths in spring. Using pieces of bent wire, pin down young growths, about 8 cm (3 in) from their tips, into shallow 5 cm (2 in) deep depressions near the parent plant. Cover the stems with lime-free potting compost, burying the pegs, but leaving the tips exposed. Keep moist until rooted, which usually takes from one to two years. When rooted, sever the young plants from their parents in spring, and leave undisturbed for another three weeks before planting out or potting up.

CHAPTER 5

PLANTING AND SUPPORTING

Having matched a plant's needs to its allocated position in the garden (see Chapter 1), planting can begin. That is assuming that the soil has been well prepared by digging in plenty of organic matter and cultivating down to a fine tilth (see Chapter 3).

> **Additional tools for planting**
> Measuring rod, 2 m (7 ft), made DIY
> Bulb planter is preferred to a trowel by some

Depth of soil Bear in mind that herbaceous border perennials, small shrubs and vegetables ideally need 25–30 cm (10–12 in) depth of good topsoil. In the vast majority of gardens the soil falls far below this standard. In the vegetable garden, where the land is vacant for part of every year, it is possible to raise the overall fertility relatively quickly – by repeatedly digging in generous quantities of organic matter prior to planting short-term crops. In permanently planted shrub and mixed borders things are more difficult, and this is why it is recommended to set out all permanent long-stay plants into pockets of good topsoil (see below). Trees and large shrubs need an even greater depth of topsoil than border perennials and small shrubs – up to 45 cm (18 in) and more. To ensure this depth of soil around their roots, they should always be set out into deeply prepared planting pits.

Planting season The ideal planting seasons for long-stay plants of any sort are autumn and spring. But container-raised stock can be set out virtually any time of year, apart from the depths of winter and the height of summer. This is provided the plants can be kept well watered and nursed along afterwards. However, don't attempt to plant when the soil is over wet or frozen, nor on heavy soil, when it is over dry. And choose a calm, dull day for preference; wind and sun can soon dry out any exposed delicate roots during the planting operation. The plants will then suffer an unnecessary setback from which they may take some time to recover.

THE ORNAMENTAL GARDEN

PLANTING LARGER TREES AND SHRUBS IN BEDS, BORDERS AND GRASS – PIT PLANTING

The plants Always buy container-raised shrubs and conifers of under 90 cm (3 ft) in height. Larger plants make greater initial impact, but they are more difficult to establish and are likely to be less rootfirm at a later date, other things being equal. Container-grown standard trees of up to 2.4 m (8 ft) should transplant satisfactorily.

Planting positions Mark out planting positions, allowing each tree or shrub a minimum space equal to its final spread, unless otherwise specified on the label. Ensure tall plants are set behind small, and remember it is the ultimate size which matters, not the size at planting time. Don't plant any tree closer to a building or drains than a distance equal to its ultimate height. You could risk damage to foundations – or broken drains.

Preparing the hole Dig out a hole at least twice as wide and half as deep again as the rootball, after first skimming off the turf in grassed areas. Keep the dark fertile topsoil separate from the less fertile, paler subsoil. Take a garden fork and loosen up the bottom and sides of the hole. Where turf is involved, turn the sods upside down in the hole and chop into small pieces. Otherwise bottom out with a 5 cm (2 in) layer of well rotted garden compost or manure (Fig. 15 *a* & *b*).

Some trees need support. If so, hammer in a stake at this stage, slightly off centre. Allow for about a third of any stake to be below ground. With standard trees, the top of the stake should come up no higher than 5 cm (2 in) below the lowest branches (Fig. 15*c*). With bushes make the stake about three quarters the height of the bush.

Scatter a small handful of general fertilizer like Growmore over the chopped turf, compost or manure. Then try the hole for size by lowering in the plant, complete with container. Underpack with 'planting mixture' until the top of the rootball rests just below the surrounding soil level (Fig. 15*d*).

Planting mixture Soil-based potting compost makes an excellent planting mixture. But if the topsoil is reasonable, it is cheaper and quite satisfactory to mix three bucketsful of this with one each of coarse sand and peat, together with a handful of general fertilizer to each 36 l (8 gal) of mix. Using a planting mixture makes it easier for the plant roots to break out of the peat-based potting compost of the nursery container, into the garden soil. It acts rather like a bridge.

Planting Water the hole thoroughly and allow surplus water to drain away. Similarly, water the containerized plant and allow it to drain before disturbing

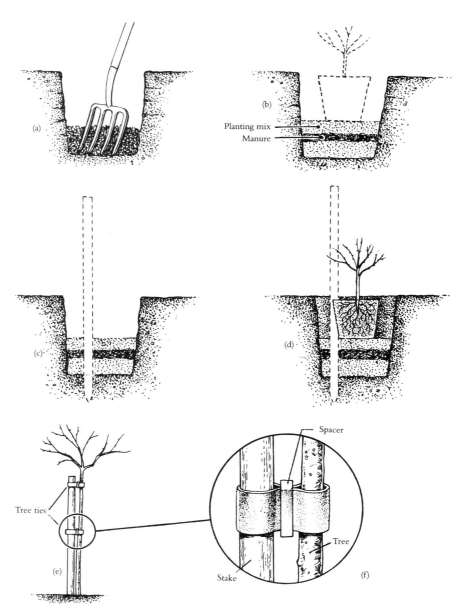

Fig. 15 Planting

a. Dig out a hole twice as wide and half as deep again as the rootball.

b. Bottom out with manure, fertilizer and planting mixture.

c. Drive in stake – if required.

d. Fit plant snugly onto the planting mixture and firm more around the roots.

e. **Staking trees** Tie trees to secure near the top and half way down.

f. Proprietary tree tie with spacer.

Break down lumps, level off and rake in dry fertilizer before sowing or planting.

the roots. In the interim, tie in the shoots of spreading kinds with soft twine to afford temporary protection, avoid breakage and make for easier planting.

The easiest way to remove floppy plastic or fibre pots is to cut vertically up both sides and peel away. Having done this, tease out some of the old potting compost with a pointed stick, along with the drainage crocks from the base. Aim to keep the main rootball intact while easing some of the outermost roots away from the rootball. This enables them to grow more quickly into the surrounding soil. Trim back to sound tissue any roots which are damaged. It is important to work quickly, as the roots must not dry out at any stage. Position the plant in the hole with its best side facing the main viewing point and its rootball resting snugly into the planting mixture. Spread out the loosened roots and backfill with more planting mixture, firming as filling proceeds. Water to settle in.

If a tree needs support, tie it to the stake in two places, near the top and about half way down. Always use proprietary tree ties with spacers to avoid chafing the bark (Fig. 15 *e* & *f*).

When planting in grass, be sure to leave a minimum 30 cm (12 in) collar of bare earth. This reduces the competition for food and moisture and enables plants to be watered and mulched effectively.

PLANTING SMALLER SHRUBS
As with large shrubs, use the 'twice as wide and half as deep again' rule as a general guideline for the size of hole. However, don't make any hole smaller than 20 cm (16 in) square by a similar depth. Otherwise there is insufficient space for working in organic matter and infilling with planting mixture. Proceed with preparations for planting and plant as described for larger shrubs.

PLANTING A HEDGE
Hedging plants over 25 cm (10 in) and under 60 cm (2 ft) in height transplant best, and should quickly form a mature hedge.

The easiest way to plant a hedge is to treat each hedging plant as a small shrub, taking out and preparing an individual planting hole for each. Peg out a straight line and insert canes as markers to indicate planting positions of a single row (a single row is adequate unless an exceptionally thick hedge is needed, when a double row can be considered). Hedging plants are normally set out at 45–60 cm (18–24 in) apart. But be guided by the recommendations on the label of the specific variety in question.

Plant the hedging and water to settle in. In exposed gardens which are inclined to be windswept, young hedging plants are going to need supporting. Either tie each plant individually to a cane pushed firmly into the ground alongside, or tie each to a taut wire running the length of the hedge and attached to posts at either end, and between as well if necessary to avoid sagging. The other alternative is to protect and shelter new hedging with wattle fencing or the like, until it is established.

PLANTING CLIMBERS AND WALL PLANTS
Don't set any wall plant or climber closer to a wall than 30 cm (12 in). The risks are excessive dryness from the plant's point of view, and possible damage to the foundations from the householders'. The same principles apply as when planting trees and shrubs: take out a hole sufficiently large to enable plenty of organic matter and planting mixture to be worked in beneath the plant, and then subsequently in and around the roots when backfilling. With smaller plants always make the hole a minimum of 30 cm (12 in) wider and 15 cm (6 in) deeper than the rootball.

Ensure adequate supports are in place before planting. Trellis of some sort is suitable for most climbers, and is essential for the likes of ivy, climbing hydrangeas and Virginia creeper, which climb by means of aerial roots and sucker pads. The danger with this type of climber is that unless grown up a trellis, they can, in time, damage the masonry. Old mortar is most at risk.

Fix the trellis onto 2.5 cm (1 in) thick blocks. These should be screwed into drilled and plugged walls. By securing the trellis 2.5 cm (1 in) out from the wall, aerial roots are kept away from the masonry and a good circulation of air is ensured, preventing moisture being trapped between climber and wall.

PLANTING IN ROCK GARDENS
Excavate pockets as deep as is practical. Bottom out with soil-based potting compost or planting mixture, using lime-free compost for lime haters. Pack more compost in and around the roots and, finally, cover over with chippings to prevent soil compaction and erosion. Use limestone chippings for lime lovers and granite for lime haters.

PLANTING ROSES
Although the majority of shrubs are sold containerized these days, roses are still often an exception. Many come in attractive prepacks, with little soil at their roots, and they need extra care when planting. The planting season for roses is from late autumn after leaf fall, on through winter during mild spells. All planting should be completed by early spring in the case of bare root plants. Container-grown roses can be set out almost any time, as with other shrubs.

Planting bushes and standards Take out planting holes and prepare as for large shrubs. Make the holes about 45 cm (18 in) wide and deep enough to accommodate the roots comfortably after bottoming out with well rotted manure or garden compost and planting mixture. Ensure that roses are always set out at the same depth as before the move. The soil mark should be visible on the stem. Soak the roots for a few hours in a bucket of clean water before planting. Trim back any which are very long, and cut back to healthy wood any which are broken, damaged or diseased. Spread out the roots and backfill as for large shrubs (Fig. 16).

With standard roses, the stakes should be in position before planting. Check that the top of the stake will end about 5 cm (2 in) below the bottom branch. After planting, tie near the top and again about half way down, using proprietary ties with spacers.

Planting climbers and ramblers Think in terms of taking out large planting holes of about 60 cm (24 in) square. This is especially important if planting against a dwelling where conditions are often too dry for roses. The larger sized hole allows for more organic matter to be forked in rather than less. As with other climbers, ensure trellis is in place prior to planting. Position the rose with its stem to the back of the planting hole and roots spread nicely round to front. Backfill as before.

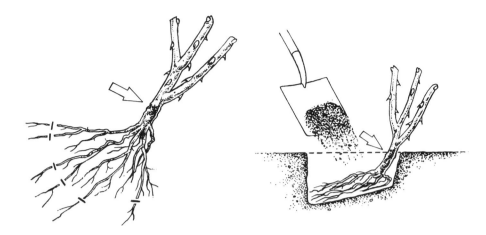

Fig. 16 Planting bare-root roses
Left. Before planting bare-root roses, trim back overlong roots.
Right. Set climbers and ramblers to the side of the hole nearest the support, with the roots well spread out.

PLANTING SHORT-STAY BEDDING PLANTS

There are two main planting seasons for short-stay bedding plants (plants which are grown for one seasonal burst of colour and then lifted). Popularly grown summer bedding plants, which flower from early summer to early autumn, are set out in early summer. And spring bedding plants which flower in the main from late winter to late spring are set out in early autumn, while there is still some warmth in the soil. In most gardens spring bedding plants very often go into land vacated by the summer varieties. Incidentally, some so-called spring bedding plants flower intermittently throughout winter in mild areas.

Bedding plants are perhaps the most vulnerable of all ornamentals at planting time. This is largely because the growth is soft and they are set out while in active growth, and in many instances when actually in flower. So extra care is needed.

Ensure the soil is well prepared (see Chapter 2). Plenty of organic matter should be incorporated during preparations. And the soil needs to be broken down into a fine crumbly tilth by forking or cultivating and raking. Immediately prior to planting, spread and rake in general fertilizer at the rate of a small handful per sq m (yd). Water thoroughly the day before planting, in all but the very wettest of weather. Use a can with a fine rose and apply at least 10 l per sq m (2 gal per sq yd), and leave to soak overnight. Similarly, soak all plants thoroughly and leave to drain for about half an hour before disturbing their roots. Most plants are sold in strips of polystyrene. Ease them apart carefully so as not to damage their roots. One good way is to cut the polystyrene and then peel it back bit by bit.

When planting for display, grade plants for ultimate height, setting short in front of tall.

Wallflowers are the one exception. These spring bedding plants are usually sold in bundles with little soil at their roots. Soak them in a bucket of clean water prior to planting.

The cool of the evening is the best time for planting. Use a trowel and take out holes large enough to take the roots comfortably. The soil should be well firmed back around the roots, using the fingers or the handle of the trowel. Water to settle the plants.

Note Before setting out bedding plants, do check on the ultimate height of the plants. Set tall behind short in front-facing borders. And in beds viewed from all sides, do ensure the tall varieties are centrally placed and surrounded by the more dwarfing kinds.

PLANTING BULBS IN BEDS AND BORDERS

Handle all bulbs with care – each is a living plant. Always aim to plant in drifts of one variety for maximum effect. And for a natural look, scatter the bulbs at random – and plant where they fall. Daffodils, narcissi, crocus and tulips are all planted in autumn.

Plant in well prepared soil, finally raking in a handful of Growmore general fertilizer per sq m (yd). Then using a trowel, take out holes slightly deeper than three times the depth of the bulbs in question; bottom out each hole with coarse sand (this is particularly important on soils inclined to be heavy); drop in the bulb, right way up, and cover with excavated soil (Fig. 17). Mark the position so that emerging shoots and roots are not damaged during the autumn/winter clean up.

SOME POINTS TO WATCH

Basin planting On very light, quick draining, sandy soils in dry climates, set plants out slightly deeper than the norm. 'Dish' the surrounding soil slightly so as to create an encircling ridge. Rain and irrigation water is then trapped and

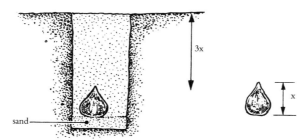

Fig. 17 Ideally set bulbs on sand. Plant at a depth equivalent to three times the depth of the bulb.

directed towards the roots where it is needed. Hedging plants can be treated individually as above when planting, or alternatively they can be set out in a 5–7.5 cm (2–3 in) deep, flat-bottomed drill.

Mound planting On low-lying wet soils in high rainfall areas, set plants out on slight mounds, about 5 cm (2 in) above the surrounding soil. And in the case of hedging, make it a continuous raised ridge.

Sloping ground It is important to ensure that the top of the rootball is not any higher than the surrounding soil when planting on sloping ground, or you risk exposed surface roots as the soil is inevitably washed down and eroded away.

PLANTING IN CONTAINERS
Never forget that it is just as important to match plant needs to the site when growing in containers as it is when planting direct into beds and borders.

The containers The size of container is very important. As a rule-of-thumb guide, set out single specimen trees or shrubs into containers two sizes up from that in which they were growing in the nursery. However, bear in mind that long-stay plants will need potting on annually into larger containers, until eventually average-sized mature trees will be growing in a container of 35–40 cm (14–16 in) in diameter. It takes a lot of compost to sustain and anchor mature trees and shrubs. Wide-based containers (wider than high) are more wind stable and less likely to blow over than tall narrow ones.

Good drainage too is vital to success, so ensure that there are plenty of drainage holes in the base of the container.

Wash, scrub and disinfect any container being reused. Soak new containers of concrete, simulated stone and terracotta in clean water for at least 24 hours before filling. This washes out any harmful salts and rehydrates the container so that it does not rob the potting compost of moisture in the early days after planting.

Planting Cover the drainage holes with fine mesh netting, wired into position to secure. This prevents the wash-through of potting compost and blocks the entry of worms, pests and insects. Bottom out containers with clean stones or broken pieces of polystyrene for drainage. Part fill with soil-based potting compost, using lime-free mixtures for lime haters like rhododendrons (Fig. 18). Peat-based composts are best reserved for short-term container plants that are going to be moved on, or disposed of, within six months. After this time, peat-based mixtures lose condition and are very difficult to manage, as indeed they are during winter.

Prepare plants for planting, as described for direct planting. Position the plant

Plant out pruned raspberry canes and firm in by treading.

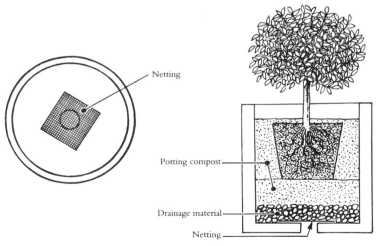

Netting

Potting compost

Drainage material

Netting

Fig. 18 Planting in containers
Left. Secure netting over drainage holes with wire before filling.
Right. Bottom out with polystyrene for drainage – part fill with soil-based potting compost, position plant, infill and firm to leave a space at the top for watering.

with rootball resting on the potting compost. Underpack with more compost so that the top of the rootball rests about 2.5 cm (1 in) below the rim of the container. Work potting compost around the sides of the rootball and firm. Topdress with more potting compost by scattering a handful or two around the stem, leaving a space of 2 cm (¾ in) for watering. Water in to settle the compost.

THE KITCHEN GARDEN

PLANTING FRUITS

Fruit trees and bushes Opt for modern dwarf varieties when buying free-standing tree fruits. Pit plant all fruits as described for ornamental trees, shrubs and climbers.

Raspberry canes Take out a trench about the depth of a spade and 45 cm (18 in) wide. Fork in a generous layer of well rotted manure or garden compost into the

Using fresh growbags each year overcomes the problem of soil preparation for tomatoes.

bottom. Replace the topsoil, breaking it down in the process.

Erect supports: hammer home a 2 m (7 ft) post at either end of the row. Make it at 3 m (10 ft) intervals in the case of a long row. Fix two wires to the posts to run along the length of the row, at 90 cm (3 ft) and 1.5 m (5 ft) above the ground respectively. The rasp canes are tied into the wires as they grow.

Rake in a handful of general fertilizer per m (yd) run of trench, and take out trowel holes deep enough and wide enough to take the rasp canes. These are usually planted at 40–60 cm (16–24 in) apart, depending on variety. After planting, firm by treading close into the stem. And cut back top growth to 25 cm (10 in).

Strawberries Prepare the ground as for short-stay bedding plants. Trowel plant and plant firmly, spacing plants about 45 cm (18 in) apart with 75 cm (30 in) between rows, and ending up with the top of the rootball level with the surrounding soil. Plant in late summer.

PLANTING VEGETABLES
It is important not to plant the same type of vegetable crop on the same piece of land more than one year in three. To do so is to risk a build up of pests and diseases.

Potatoes Take out 15 cm (6 in) deep flat-bottomed drills on land that has been previously dug, manured and well cultivated. Allow about 60 cm (24 in) between rows. Apply fertilizer into the bottom of the drills at the rate of a small handful per m (yd) run. Set the potatoes about 30 cm (12 in) apart for early varieties; set maincrop varieties slightly wider apart, and always with their 'eyes' or shoots uppermost. Return the soil, breaking it up finely and forming a slight ridge. Do not firm. The earliest varieties are planted during early spring in mild areas and in mid-spring in cold districts. Maincrop varieties are planted about a fortnight later.

Runner beans Indoor raised plants are hardened off and planted out in early summer. Prepare and fertilize the trench as for raspberry canes (see page 63), but make it 60 cm (24 in) wide. Runner beans are usually planted out in a double row with 45 cm (18 in) between the two rows and 30 cm (12 in) between plants within the rows.

Erect supports prior to planting. Runner beans are usually trained up pairs of bean poles. These are crossed and tied together about 15 cm (6 in) from the top, with their bottoms pushed firmly into the ground to coincide with the proposed plant spacings. One plant is set at the base of each pole. To give stability, tie a final pole horizontally along the top. Trowel plant, ensuring that the roots are comfortably spread before backfilling.

Brassicas – cabbage, cauliflowers and brussels sprouts Plant on land which has previously been dug deeply, manured well and limed. Rake in a handful of general fertilizer per sq m (yd) prior to planting, and firm the soil by treading. These crops need a firm, well settled bed. Trowel plant firmly, as deep as the first seed leaves. Space plants 60–75 cm (24–30 in) apart both ways, depending on variety.

Lettuce Prepare the ground as for brassicas. Lettuce too like well limed soil. Set the plants 25–30 cm (10–12 in) apart, depending on variety. Trowel plant reasonably firmly, but not as firmly as the brassicas.

Tomatoes These are tender plants, needing a favoured, warm, sheltered spot and soil of above average fertility. Therefore it is recommended to plant tomatoes in containers of potting compost, as described for trees and shrubs (see page 53). And give them priority for a sunny, sheltered spot on the patio. Standard varieties will need a cane for support. The other alternative is to plant in growbags. Ensure plenty of drainage slits in the base and support with proprietary plant frame supports.

Leeks are usually planted early to mid-summer. Prepare the ground and fertilize as for annual short-stay plants. Take out a shallow trench with a draw hoe. Trim the top quarter of the leaves off the leek plants. Make dibber holes about 15–25 cm (6–10 in) apart along the bottom of the trench. Drop the plants in as deep as the base of their leaves. Water in but do not firm. Leave it to rain, and for irrigation water gradually to wash down the soil.

Onion sets and shallots Prepare the ground, lime and firm as for the brassicas (see above). Trowel plant onion sets firmly, 20 cm (8 in) apart both ways; allow half as much again for the shallots. Bury both shallots and onion sets so that their tops are just showing, otherwise they will almost certainly be uprooted by birds. Early to mid-spring is the average planting time.

Marrows Choosing a warm, sheltered spot, dig out a 60 cm (2 ft) square pocket. Make it to the depth of a spade and set the soil to one side. Fork two or three bucketsful of well rotted compost or manure into the bottom of the excavated pocket. Scatter over a very small handful of general fertilizer. Return the topsoil, breaking it up in the process and forming a raised bed. Rake in another very small handful of general fertilizer. Trowel plant one plant per mound after all danger of frost has passed in early summer.

Note Don't lime any one particular piece of ground in the vegetable garden more than one year in three.

CHAPTER 6

SIMPLE PRUNING AND TRAINING

Tools

Hand pruners/secateurs	Long arm pruner
Knife	Garden shears
Pruning saw	Hedge trimmer

THE BASICS

Having a good understanding of why pruning and training are necessary is a major step towards success. What are the aims and objects?

Pruning is carried out:
    to train and maintain shape and form.
    to improve and maintain plant health and prolong life.
    to regulate and sustain cropping and flowering.

Pruning normally has the effect of stimulating growth and is all about the timely cutting out and removal of shoots or parts of shoots or roots. Generally speaking, hard pruning – severe cutting back – of a plant will result in vigorous new growth. This is accompanied, at least in the short term, by some slight delay in flowering and fruiting. Expect fewer but higher quality flowers and fruits to be produced over a longer period with hard pruning. The aim for average purposes should be to steer a middle course when pruning. And it is important that the severity of pruning is not viewed in isolation. It needs to be related to feeding and general management to get a balanced picture.

TIMING

The timing of pruning is important from various viewpoints.

DECIDUOUS TREES AND SHRUBS
These are best pruned in late summer or autumn. As a rule, spring pruning is best avoided. This is particularly true of deciduous ornamental trees, many of which are severely weakened by being cut at this time of year.

EVERGREENS

Conifers included, these are normally best pruned in late spring or summer. This minimizes the risk of frost or wind injury which can otherwise arise, especially if pruned in winter.

HEDGES

Hedges of all kinds, deciduous and evergreen, are best trimmed in summer or early autumn when the shoots are green, soft and easy to cut. By letting in more air at this time of year the remaining wood is also better able to ripen. This in turn greatly improves the resistance to winter injury. However, it is often more practical to deal with badly neglected deciduous hedges in early winter after leaf fall, when it is easier to see where to make the cuts.

'SANITATION' PRUNING

This refers to the cutting out – or shortening back to sound wood – of dead, damaged or badly diseased growths, and is best carried out as soon as possible after discovery, regardless of the time of year, frosty weather excepted. This reduces the risk of further possible disease infection spreading into healthy tissue.

FROSTY WEATHER

Never prune during hard frosts when you risk wood splitting, with the consequential entry of disease.

PRUNING CUTS

The first fundamental rule when making any pruning cut, regardless of size, is that it is clean. There must be no suggestion of jagged edges or tearing. In order to achieve these ends, it is essential that all pruning tools are clean, sharp, well maintained and with all moving parts suitably lubricated.

When pruning back to a bud, start the cut on the opposite side of the stem to the bud and slightly lower down. Then angle the cut so as to make a sloping finish – ending up about 3 mm (⅛ in) above the top of the bud (Fig. 19).

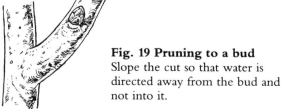

Fig. 19 Pruning to a bud
Slope the cut so that water is directed away from the bud and not into it.

STOPPING/PINCHING

These are the terms variously used to describe the removal of growing points. Plants are normally 'stopped' with the intention of encouraging the development of sideshoots and branching below the cut. Take a sharp knife to remove the growing tip and take it out just above a good bud or leaf joint. For the removal of very soft growing points, some old hands prefer to use their thumb nail. But until experience is gained, use a knife – and pruners if the wood is hard.

CLIPPING

Clipping is normally reserved for formal effects – hedges, topiary and bushes included. In this situation, cut back all new growth. Trim to a uniform length and back to within 6–12 mm (¼–½ in) of the older wood with shears or hedge trimmer. The result is that secondary shoots break away and a dense texture is created.

HEADING BACK

Heading back (de-horning or crown reduction) involves the shortening back of all the main stems and branches, so reducing the overall height and spread of the crown. Shrubs and trees are often headed back when they have outgrown their allotted space.

Slender shoots of up to 2 cm (¾ in) in thickness are cut back to a healthy outward pointing bud or sideshoot. Thicker branches have their tips shortened back to a strong secondary branch. Avoid shortening back any individual branch by more than one third its length.

THINNING

This is the answer where the crowns of trees and shrubs have been allowed to become overcrowded, or where a more open texture is the aim. In both cases up to one third of the sideshoots and branches are selectively cut out. Each one is taken back to a main branch, stem or bud.

LOPPING

Lopping involves saw work. And when dealing with trees any work above about 2 m (7 ft) is best left to the professionals. Safety harnesses are needed; experience and training required.

However, the removal of old dead or outworn lower branches, up to about 7.5 cm (3 in) in diameter, can reasonably be tackled by the fit and able working from ground level. Branches of up to about 1.8 m (6 ft) in length can be removed intact. Anything longer is best taken out in sections of say about 1.2 m (4 ft) lengths. This reduces the risk of accidents, of wood splitting back into the main framework and of possible damage to underplanting.

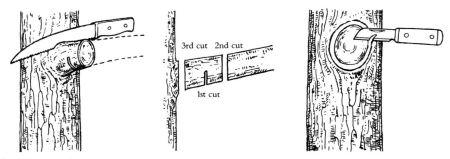

Fig. 20 Lopping
Left. When removing the final section of a branch:
1. Cut one-quarter way through on the underside.
2. Cut down from above – 2.5 cm (1 in) out from the first cut.
3. Trim back the short stump, flush with the main stem.
Right. Smooth off rough edges with a sharp knife and paint over with sealant.

To remove a branch, or the final section of a branch, cut about quarter way through the limb on the underside – some 10 cm (4 in) out from the trunk/main stem. Then cut down from the topside about 12.5 cm (5 in) out from the trunk/main stem, completely severing the branch and leaving a short stump. Finally cut off the short stump, flush with the trunk or main stem. Cut down from above and smooth off any rough edges with a sharp knife (Fig. 20). Paint over all saw cuts with a proprietary sealant paint to encourage healing and prevent the entry of disease organisms. Undercutting a branch helps to prevent splitting and consequential disease entry.

PRUNING TOOLS

A GOOD PAIR OF HAND PRUNERS/SECATEURS
If clean, sharp and well maintained, there is little to choose between the anvil and side anvil/by-pass models. Most will normally cut wood up to 1 cm (½ in) thick, and up to 2 cm (¾ in) with heavy duty models. Opt for the best within your budget.

A STRONG, SHARP KNIFE
As very few people have the time, expertise or inclination to sharpen knives, there is much to be said in favour of models which take replacement blades.

A PRUNING SAW
A curved or narrow-bladed pruning saw – one intended to cut green wood – will be needed where anything over 2 cm (¾ in) needs cutting.

A LONG ARM PRUNER

Where there is a fair amount of pruning above about 1.8 m (6 ft) in height, a lightweight alloy, long arm pruner will be found to be indispensable.

GARDEN SHEARS/POWERED HEDGE TRIMMER

In the right hands a good pair of garden shears will cope with up to about a 6 m (20 ft) run of clipped hedge. For greater lengths of hedging, a powered hedge trimmer is invaluable. Before buying an electric hedge trimmer, ensure that the hedge is within easy and safe reach of the mains supply, and always use with a safety power breaker.

Deadhead roses as the flowers fade, to ensure continuity of bloom.

ROUTINE PRUNING OF ORNAMENTAL TREES

AND SHRUBS

Never neglect pruning. The ideal is to prune while the branches are small. This avoids making big cuts later on.

Pre- and immediate post-planting pruning As a general rule, little pruning is needed before planting, apart from shortening damaged or overlong roots back to sound tissue. But any dead, damaged or overlong shoots should also be shortened back to a good healthy outward pointing bud as a matter of course.

Routine maintenance of deciduous ornamental garden trees Most get by with relatively little pruning, provided they have room to grow. The majority are best pruned in summer or autumn. Pruning in the early years is largely a matter of selectively thinning out any overcrowded, crossing, inward growing, damaged or diseased branches. Aim to maintain a fairly open framework.

Routine maintenance of evergreen trees, including conifers As a general rule these trees require minimal pruning, but if necessary it should be attended to in summer. It is usually a case of shortening back any straggly, untidy or misplaced shoots, together with sanitation pruning if required.

One of the most important pruning tasks with any single-stemmed conifer is to prevent forking of the main stem. Remove any secondary main leaders as they develop. Leave only one – the strongest and the straightest.

As with deciduous trees, remove the bottom branches of older trees as and when they obviously come to the end of their useful life.

PRUNING SHRUBS

Routine maintenance of shrubs With any shrub begin by shortening back or cutting out dead, dying, damaged or diseased growths back to a good bud, sideshoot, branch or trunk. At the same time, cut out inward growing, crossing, straggly, untidy, misplaced and, in the case of non-weeping plants, downward-growing shoots. Then deal with suckers and reverted green shoots.

Many suckers are unwanted growths which arise at or near soil level or, in the case of standards, higher up the stem. They are commonplace on shrubs which have been budded or grafted during propagation, so that a superior gardenworthy variety can be grown on the roots of another closely related plant. Sometimes after budding or grafting suckers break away from the roots. These need to be ruthlessly cut back, as near as possible to their point of origin. If left unchecked they will take over, smothering out the sought after main plant growth. Shrubs such as roses and rhododendrons are among the most likely to have suckers.

But not all suckers are bad. Some shrubs, including kerria and hypericum, along with fruits like raspberries, have a natural suckering habit. They produce suckers identical to the parent, and these suckers are suitable to detach for propagating purposes.

Reverted shoots are inferior growths which arise amidst the foliage. They are frequently to be found in variegated trees, shrubs and climbers. Strong-growing reverted green shoots appear amongst the variegated. Cut these out promptly, back to their point of origin. Otherwise they will soon crowd out the less vigorous variegated foliage.

Although many shrubs will grow and put on a good show of flower and foliage colour with nothing more than the above routine treatment, many respond to a regular programme of more specialist pruning. And for pruning purposes, most shrubs can be categorized into certain, fairly clearly defined groups, according to their flowering habit and pruning needs. When in doubt as to the flowering or fruiting habit of a shrub, don't start cutting immediately. It is much better to watch it closely, for twelve months if need be, and establish which wood carriers the flowers and fruits and at what time of year.

Group A Shrubs which usually flower in spring or summer, on wood formed the previous year. These shrubs are pruned immediately after flowering is over for the season. Cut back all flowered wood to one or two buds. Leave the bulk of the new season's growth alone, as it is needed to replace the spent wood and carry the following year's flowers. However, cut out any weak new shoots.

Some of these shrubs are more easily dealt with by clipping over with shears at about 90% flower fall. A formally treated forsythia is a good example of a shrub which responds well to this treatment.

Group B Shrubs which flower mainly during summer, on both new season's growths as well as on wood formed in the previous year. Selectively thin these shrubs immediately after flowering. Remove up to slightly more than half of the previous season's flowered wood. Also cut out the weakest of the new shoots; then shorten back new growths by one third to half their length. With berrying shrubs like pyracantha, selectively thin out fruited wood in spring instead of at flowering time, otherwise much of the berrying effect will be lost.

Group C Shrubs which flower in late summer and autumn at the tips of new season's growths. Shorten all flowered wood back to within one or two buds of the main framework in late winter or early spring. This encourages an abundance of new flowering stems.

Group D Naturally neat and slow growing shrubs, requiring little or no pruning apart from shortening untidy, straggly or misplaced growths. Often young shrubs belonging to this group – rhododendrons and azaleas for example – benefit from deadheading immediately after flowering for the first few years. Remove the old flower heads back to just above a leaf. And in the case of rhododendrons and azaleas, take care not to damage the following year's buds which are situated at the base of the spent blooms.

Group E Shrubs which are grown mainly for foliage effect and respond to clipping. Evergreens are best clipped in late spring or summer. Deciduous varieties are normally best cut in late summer or autumn. In the case of shrubs with large leaves, take a pair of hand pruners and cut through stems rather than leaves. This avoids the problem of bruised and sliced leaves – and the resulting unsightliness of discolouration at the cut edges.

PRUNING ROSES

Types Roses come in a bewildering range of types, varieties, shapes and forms. However, for pruning purposes they can be narrowed down to four main types.
Bush varieties are made up of the ever popular HT (Hybrid Tea) or LF (Large Flowered) varieties, plus the floribunda or CF (Cluster Flowered) kinds. Many of these varieties are also grown as single-stemmed standards.
Climbers and ramblers can be lumped together for practical pruning purposes, although the keen rosarian may prefer to consider them as two distinct groups.
Shrub roses make up a pretty variable group. Only the modern shrub roses are considered here.
Miniatures These are dwarf varieties which produce miniature flowers. They are perfect replicas of their larger-flowered relatives.

Pruning at planting time Immediately before planting out, root prune as for any other shrub. Then treat as follows:
Bush roses After autumn planting, shorten back the shoots by about one third their length. In spring both these autumn-planted roses and spring-planted roses are dealt with in a similar manner. Shorten back all growths to within about 15 cm (6 in) of the ground, provided this leaves four or five good buds. Otherwise don't cut back quite so hard.
Climbers and ramblers are pruned more lightly, cutting back main stems to a good bud but within about 45 cm (18 in) of the ground. Any weak growths are cut down to within 10 cm (4 in) of the ground.
Shrub roses and miniatures have their shoots shortened back by about half their length in late winter or early spring.

Subsequent pruning

Bush roses flower on the tips of new season's shoots and in consequence are hard pruned in late winter or early spring, as signs of new growth become evident.

HT/LF varieties have the previous season's wood cut back to within about three buds of the older wood. Floribunda/CF roses, being more vigorous than HT/LF varieties, are pruned more lightly, to within about five buds.

Standard varieties are pruned in a similar way. Simply treat the top as a bush HT or floribunda, as appropriate.

Deadheading is important. As soon as the flowers start to fade, remove the old flower heads or clusters, back to just above a good leaf. This encourages prolonged flowering. In autumn, shorten back all new growths by about one third their length. This enables plants to withstand better the winter buffetting by wind, and takes them safely through to the main pruning season in spring.

Climbers Tie in the first formed main stems to a support of some kind to create a basic framework of branches. Climbers bloom on new season's shoots and are autumn pruned. Shorten back all new growths to within about two buds of the main framework. When strong new growths arise from the base, take the opportunity to cut out the weakest of the main stems, back to near ground level, and tie in the new growths as replacements. Deadhead as for bush varieties.

Ramblers Unlike climbers, there is no permanent framework. Ramblers normally flower on wood formed the previous year. These varieties are summer pruned as soon as flowering is over for the season. Cut out flowered wood, back to its point of origin, and then tie in new vigorous, healthy, replacement growths. During the course of the growing season, new growths should be loosely tied into canes, unobtrusively pushed in alongside. This protects them from damage and makes autumn tying in a great deal easier.

Modern shrub roses flower on both new and old wood. They are pruned in late winter or early spring when the previous season's wood is shortened back by about a third. Cut out any dead, damaged, diseased, weak or crossing wood at the same time. In addition mature shrubs should have about one fifth of the old wood cut out each year, in strict rotation. Deadhead shrub roses, unless rose hips are a feature of the variety, in which case leave well alone.

Miniature roses flower on young wood. They are cut back by about half in late winter or early spring. During summer, regular deadheading is called for to ensure continuous flowering.

TRIMMING A FORMAL HEDGE

NEW HEDGES

Deciduous During the first dormant season after planting, cut hedging plants back by about half their height. This encourages the sought after new growth

from low down. Leave to grow on for a full season without further pruning.
Broad–leaved evergreens Treat in a similar manner to deciduous kinds, but
cut back less hard and confine pruning to summer.
Conifers Require no initial pruning.

YOUNG AND ESTABLISHED HEDGES

Deciduous During the formative years don't try to achieve hedge height too
quickly. After each 20 cm (8 in) of growth has been made, shorten back the new
shoots by about a third their length. This usually involves clipping two or three
times a year. At the same time clip in the sides, always keeping the top of the
hedge slightly narrower than the base. This way you avoid bareness in the lower
regions, due to lack of light. Once the required hedge height is reached – it takes
on average from three to five years – deciduous hedges are ideally clipped back

Tie in new season's raspberry canes to supporting wires, allowing 10 cm (4 in) minimum
space between each cane.

to shape in summer and again in autumn. The final trim should take the new growth back to within 2.5 cm (1 in) of older wood.

Broad-leaved evergreens Trim in summer and slightly less hard than for deciduous hedges. Once hedge height is reached, growth rate determines the number of times the hedge is clipped. This is much more variable than with deciduous kinds – ranging from one to four cuts a season.

Conifer hedges Don't cut out the tops until the plants have reached the required hedge height. But do lightly trim in regularly at the sides.

PRUNING FRUIT TREES

Fruit pruning is something of a specialist subject, and becomes ever more diverse as new varieties of familiar fruits come on stream. To add to the confusion, new and hitherto quite unknown fruits are coming to the fore. For the purposes of this book, it has been assumed, rightly or wrongly, that most householders usually start with well tried fruits that are reliable and easy to manage. It has also been assumed, in all cases, that the starting point is a part-trained specimen.

APPLES

Apple trees, regardless of whether they are dessert or cooking varieties, come in a number of forms, which have differing pruning needs. They are:

Traditional free-standing bush and pyramid forms and standards, including 'family trees'.

Various intensive or wall-trained forms such as cordon, fan and espalier.

The so-called genetic dwarfs and non-branching varieties.

Planting time

Bush and standard apples Root prune as for shrubs. Immediately after autumn planting, shorten all new season's growths back by about half, to an outward pointing bud. When spring planting, it is a case of shortening back the previous season's growths. At the same time, shorten any damaged roots back to sound tissue and cut out inward growing stems.

Intensive fruit forms Cordons, fans and espaliers do not normally require top pruning at planting time.

Genetic dwarfs are not top pruned at planting time.

Subsequent pruning

Traditional free-standing bush, pyramid and standard apples Ideally prune in autumn or early winter. The normal practice is to shorten the main branch tips, taking off about a quarter of the current season's growth. Cut other sideshoots back to within about three buds of the older wood. And as before, shorten any dead, damaged or crossing branches.

Intensive forms of apples are best pruned in mid to late summer, starting when the first sideshoots reach about 30 cm (12 in) in length. Summer pruning then continues over a period of about a month – until the last of the sideshoots has reached 30 cm (12 in). Each sideshoot is shortened back to within about three buds of the older wood. At the same time the tips of the main branches are shortened back by about a quarter, to a good bud. In autumn shorten any subsequent growths near the top – back to one bud.

Genetic dwarfs and non-branching forms need minimal pruning, apart from shortening back any sideshoots to about 2.5 cm (1 in), cutting back to a good bud in summer.

PEARS

Pears are normally grown as free-standing bushes or standards, and as intensive cordons, espaliers and fans. Pruning is as for apples.

PLUMS

In the average garden, plums, gages and damsons are normally grown as free-standing bushes or half-standards. Wall-trained forms are obtainable, but they are tricky to manage and need considerable attention.

Root prune at planting time, as for any other fruit. Bush and half-standard forms then require relatively little subsequent pruning, apart from cutting out or shortening back dead, crossing or rubbing branches. Any pruning that becomes necessary should be dealt with in late summer, when the risk of infection from silver leaf disease is at its lowest ebb.

CHERRY

Varieties of sweet cherry are pruned very much as for plum, and they are pruned at the same time.

PRUNING BERRY FRUITS

SUMMER FRUITING RASPBERRIES

These are amongst the most popular of berry fruits and are easy to prune.

At planting time Root prune, then immediately after planting, cut down each cane to a good bud about 25 cm (10 in) above ground.

Subsequent pruning In the first year after planting, limit the number of new canes to each stool/rootclump to about five of the strongest. Remove the remainder during summer, along with any which appear between the rows. Cut them all off cleanly at soil level.

In the second and subsequent summers, cut out all fruited canes to ground level as soon as cropping ceases, and at the same time limit the number of new canes to no more than eight per stool – tying them in to supporting wires. In late winter, cut off the tips of each cane at about 1.5 m (5 ft).

BLACKCURRANTS
Blackcurrants produce the best fruits on young wood, and pruning is carried out with this in mind.

At planting time Root prune. Immediately after planting, cut down newly planted bushes to about 5 cm (2 in) above ground, taking each stem back to a good, outward-pointing bud.
Subsequent pruning In the second and third years, thin out any weak new growths, cutting them out at or near soil level. In later year, immediately fruit picking is finished, cut out about one third of the total number of stems each years, down to ground level. Take out the oldest wood first.

RED- AND WHITECURRANTS
Red- and whitecurrants carry their fruits on a framework of permanent branches, either on bushes or on cordons. For average purposes, bushes are easier to manage, are cheaper to buy, and crop more heavily on a plant to plant basis.

At planting time Root prune. Then after planting shorten all the main branches back by about half their length.
Subsequent pruning Each year, as soon as fruit picking is over, shorten all sideshoots back to within two buds of the main wood. Then turn to the tips of each branch and shorten back new season's growths by half.

GOOSEBERRIES
The pruning of gooseberries is carried out in much the same way as for redcurrants, with one main difference – the sideshoots are shortened back less severely to three buds and not two.

BLACKBERRIES AND HYBRID BERRIES, INCLUDING LOGANBERRIES
At planting time Root prune and shorten the top growth back to 25 cm (10 in) after planting.
Subsequent pruning In the first year, tie in new fruiting rods. Thereafter, cut out all the old fruited rods each year as soon as fruit picking is finished, and tie in new growths. These new rods should be loosely tied into canes during the growing season. This prevents them getting damaged and makes the autumn tying in a great deal easier.

CHAPTER 7

LAWNS AND LAWN CARE

Tools	
Lawnmower	Edging shears
Spring tine wire rake	Sieve
Half moon edging iron	

A well kept lawn is an asset in any garden; grass makes a safe and economical ground cover. However, it does have limitations. It will not stand up to very heavy use; and it is not suitable for paths, patios and barbecue areas where it suffers badly, especially during wet or frosty weather. One of the basic rules of lawn care is never to walk over the lawn any more than absolutely necessary when it is over-wet, nor when it is frozen or covered with snow. And if you are using your wheelbarrow under adverse conditions like these, put down planks first.

For really heavy wear, opt for hardwearing materials like concrete, bricks or tarmac. Gravel or loose chippings are best avoided in close proximity to the lawn. Chippings are inevitably kicked onto the grass where they fly dangerously when mowing and damage mower blades into the bargain.

If a lawn is to be kept looking good, it must have a certain amount of care and attention. Basic guidelines on lawn care and putting down a lawn are spelt out in the following pages. Although few householders will attempt to put down a complete lawn, most will be concerned at some time with lawn extensions and grassing over flower beds. The procedures are the same.

NEW LAWNS

SEEDING OR TURFING?

Seeding is cheaper than turfing, but there is a time lag to consider. A lawn seeded down in early autumn won't be ready for use until the following spring, and it will take little wear for 12 months thereafter. So, where there are children and pets to consider, turfing is the practical solution, as it is on heavy clay soils. Turf gives instant effect and is ready for use within a few weeks. But common sense is called for – only light wear for a while. Be mindful of the lifting involved in turfing and the actual weight of the turves. Turfing a lawn is heavy work by any standards and make it a two-person job if possible.

PREPARING THE SOIL

Preparatory work for seeding and turfing follow similar lines. In both instances a bed of well prepared topsoil of 10 cm (4 in) minimum depth is essential for success.

Start at least three months before the lawn is to be made. Having seen to drainage and levelling (page 18), dig over the plot. Remove stones and the roots of persistent weeds in the process, and don't dig too deeply (you shouldn't disturb the subsoil). Check that any part of the lawn butting up against the house is well below the damp proof course. Check that levels are slightly above existing paths, for ease of mowing. When preparing for turfing, take into account the fact that turves will be about 4 cm (1½ in) thick.

Allow the soil to settle for a few weeks, then fork a bucket of peat and half a bucket of sand per sq m (yd), into the top 15 cm (6 in) of soil. When dealing with heavy soils, double the amount of peat and sand.

Let the soil weather. Then start to level and firm, along the following lines. Rake over the area, removing all stones of any significant size and working the soil down to a fine crumb structure, while levelling out humps and hollows. Follow the raking by treading heel-to-toe fashion, to firm. Treading is better than using a roller, which tends to ride over air pockets (very often remedial treatment is needed later on to level out the hollows). Repeat the firming and raking several times, but only during dry weather when the soil is not wet.

Two weeks before seeding or turfing, rake in general fertilizer like Growmore, at the rate of a handful per sq m (yd). The site should now be ready. *Note* Banks steeper than one in three should not be grassed – this is in the interests of safe mowing. Steep banks are better terraced behind retaining walls, or planted up with ground cover. Seek professional advice.

TURFING

Spring and autumn are the best times to lay turf, but turves can be laid any time during the growing season, provided supplies are available, and provided the lawn can be nursed along afterwards, especially during periods of drought when watering becomes essential.

Mark out the area, using a line and pegs for straight edges and a trickle of sand for curves. Always work from a plank to consolidate and level and avoid leaving foot indentations on the prepared soil.

Begin at a corner and lay turves in a straight line lengthwise. Stagger the rows like brickwork so that the joins do not align (Fig. 21). Push each turf up firmly against its neighbour and tamp down gently with the back of the spade. Never use force. Any unevenness should be corrected by adding or removing soil beneath the turves, so raising or lowering individual turves as need be. Check critical levels with straight edge and spirit level. As work proceeds, rest the plank on previously laid turves and work from this. On slopes, hold turves in place by

Fig. 21 Turfing
Brush potting compost well into the gaps between turves after laying.

driving in 12 mm (½ in) diameter pegs of about 15 cm (6 in) in length, as soon as each turf is laid.

Finally, trickle potting compost into the gaps between the turves. Brush this well in and it will help to prevent drying out and shrinkage around the edges of the turves, while encouraging them to knit together quickly.

Edging Cut around the edges of the newly turved lawn, using a spade or half moon edging iron. Use a plank as a guide for straight lines. The edges of a lawn should be cut down at right angles to the surface to form a shoulder. Anything less than perpendicular will create problems later on when routine trimming. Aim for a small dip of about 5 cm (2 in) where lawn meets flower bed.

Water lawns thoroughly after turfing and keep moist until established, otherwise drying out and shrinkage back at the edges is inevitable.
Note Turves should not be left standing around after delivery. Aim to lay them within 24–48 hours or risk deterioration.

SEEDING

The best times to sow seed are mid-spring, after the soil has had a chance to warm up, and in early autumn while there is still some warmth in the soil. In cool or wet areas sowing times are therefore confined to relatively short periods, and turfing may be a better bet.

Choose a lawn seed to suit the garden. Go for a general purpose mixture for a hardwearing lawn. There is little point in sowing a fine lawn mixture and expecting it to stand up to children's wear – it won't. There are other considerations too. Is a shade mixture needed for example? Seed dressed with bird repellant is usually worth the extra cost. Allow 50 g of seed per sq m (1½ oz per sq yd).

To help ensure an even distribution of seed, divide the lawn into strips of equal size, using pegs and string or a trickle of sand. After mixing the seed with twice its volume of dry sand (this makes sowing much easier), weigh it out. Then divide the allocation for each strip into two – sowing half evenly up and down the strip and the remainder across. Lightly rake the seed in and, to avoid the all too common mistake of raking too deeply, keep the handle of the rake near to the vertical. The alternative is to cover the seed by scattering over a mixture of equal parts potting compost and sand. In any event this is the best way to deal with heavy soils.

Protect the newly seeded lawn from birds by criss-crossing dark wool over the top. Tie the wool to pegs around the edges, to keep it raised some 7.5 cm (3 in) above the surface. Don't use thread, which can cut and injure birds' feet. Wool will tip the wings and scare the birds without causing injury. Keep the seed moist until growing away nicely.

Post-seeding care

Cutting When spring sown lawns have made about 5 cm (2 in) of growth, handpick stones and then roll lightly. The rear roller of a mower serves the purpose well, keeping the cutter head clear of the seedling grasses. Leave for a few days then give the first trim. Tip off only the top 12 mm (½ in) of grass. For a good job, tipping over with hand shears cannot be bettered; however, in practice most of us risk using the mower. The blades must be set high and they must be sharp but, even so, some of the grasses are bound to be uprooted.

A newly seeded lawn should not be used until it has been lightly rolled, and cut two or three times.

In the case of autumn sown lawns, tip them over if significant growth is made during the first five weeks after sowing. Otherwise leave well alone until spring. But during winter be ever watchful for disease and treat with fungicide at the first signs of trouble.

Don't subject a newly seeded lawn to heavy wear for the first 12 months. And if those all too familiar cracks and crevices are to be avoided, aim to keep it well watered.

Edging Don't be too hasty to edge a newly seeded lawn. Let it firm up for about six months, allowing the grasses to bind the soil. Then edge as for turfing.

ESTABLISHED LAWNS

CHOOSING A MOWER

Some general points to watch for:

Power source An electric mower of some sort is the norm for most households. Hand push mowers give a good cut, but need energetic operators with a

If left unchecked, weeds will eventually smother out fine lawn grasses.

willingness to mow regularly. Petrol mowers are needed on large lawns, where trailing cables are both restrictive and dangerous.

Cylinder v. rotary mowers Traditional cylinder mowers still do the best job, but they are not suitable for rough grass or steep banks. Wheel mounted rotary mowers with rollers make a good second best. Hover mowers, which float on a cushion of air, will encourage a puffy sward unless used in conjunction with a roller. However, they are lightweight and excellent for banks, rough grass and verges. Strimmers are useful for cutting grass at the base of walls, trees and the like.

Mower size Don't skimp on size of mower. Very small machines are put under considerable strain on large lawns. Under these circumstances they cannot be expected to have a long life nor do a good job. A 30 cm (12 in) mower is about right for a lawn of up to 83 sq m (100 sq yds).

Grass collection All grass clippings are best boxed/bagged off. Failure to do this spreads weeds and moss, encourages worms and disease and builds up 'thatch' (matted grass). And there is the added nuisance of trampling grass into the home. If mowing without a grass box, pay particular attention to scarifying.

All cylinder mowers and most wheel mounted rotaries offer efficient grass collection facilities. And there is at least one hover which claims to do an acceptable job of grass collection.

Note The more expensive of the rotary mowers without grass collecting facility pulverize the grass down so finely as to have the minimum adverse effect. But don't allow the grass to grow too long between cuts.

Safety When extension leads are needed for electric mowers, go for those in dispensers which are designed for the job. This is both in the interests of safety and ease of operation. Always use an RCD cut-out plug or adaptor with an electric mower, so that if faults develop the power is cut off instantly. Although most machines are fitted with safety cut outs, some are not – avoid these. Plastic bladed rotaries are much safer than metal.

MOWING

Height of cut The height of cut should be adjusted to suit the weather and the time of year. Generally speaking, set the mower blades high for the first two or three cuts in spring. Gradually lower the height of cut until mid–summer droughts, when too close a cut puts the grasses under great stress, and height of cut should once more be raised. Cut closely again in late summer, finally raising the height of cut as cold weather approaches.

Mowing too close weakens grasses, scars and scalps, so allowing weeds and mosses to get a hold. Not mowing close enough leads to a thin sward of coarse grass. Where the grass has been allowed to grow too long, take it down gradually in stages. Make the first cut with mower set high – lowering the setting for the second and subsequent cuts made a few days later.

Frequency of mowing Start cutting in spring as soon as the grass is growing freely – a couple of cuts in early spring is usual, and no more, otherwise the grass will suffer irreparable damage should late severe frosts strike. Mow at least once a week during the main growing season. Ease off during mid–autumn and stop by late autumn.

Direction Aim to alter the direction of cut at each mowing. Mow up and down one week, across the next, and diagonally the next.

Edging After mowing, trim the edges. Long-handled edging shears are ideal but ordinary hand shears will suffice. Edges between lawn and path should be trimmed regularly with a spade or half moon edging iron. In fact all edges benefit from being recut with a spade or edging iron once a season.

ROLLING

Roll in moderation to consolidate the soil back around plant roots and so increase drought resistance. Lightly roll in spring if the lawn is puffy following the frost heave of winter; in autumn where a rollerless mower has been used throughout the season and puffiness is in evidence; new lawns before mowing for the first time.

WATERING

When establishing a new lawn, aim to have a supply of rainwater to hand as an insurance against restrictions (see page 36). Thereafter concentrate on maintaining or improving the general health of the lawn, and so its drought resistance. Sprinklers will undoubtedly keep a lawn green, but are wasteful of water.

FEEDING

Lawn feeding in spring or early summer is sound practice, annually or in alternate years. Use a proprietary balanced lawn fertilizer, suited to the time of year. Topdressing with potting compost is recommended too. These are measures designed to build up the general fertility of the lawn and are particularly important on sandy, free draining ground.

Only feed in autumn if the lawn is very impoverished, or if feeding was missed in spring. It is vital to use feed formulated for autumn use and it must go on in early autumn. If feed is given too late and a mild spell follows, there is a risk of lush, disease-prone growth.

Well-timed feeds increase disease resistance; ill-timed feeds can be harmful.

LIMING

If extreme acidity is suspected – lichen, surface blue-black slime and algae are pointers to trouble – spread ground limestone in early winter. Apply at the rate of a handful per 2 sq m (yds), but don't overdo it as lawn grasses need slightly acid soil. Too much lime encourages clovers and earthworms, and may cause the grass to yellow.

RAKING AND SCARIFYING

The best times to scarify are autumn and spring. Scarifying is always recommended before topdressing. Rake fairly vigorously over the entire lawn, using a wire rake and aiming to tease out all the old matted grass down at the roots. This allows air to circulate more freely around the base of grasses, stimulates the production of sideshoots and so thickens up the sward. First rake up and down the lawn, then mow, then rake and mow across the line of the first sweep.

Scarifying is vital in autumn where a mower without grass collection facility has been used throughout the season. Fail to scarify under these circumstances and there is a real risk of diseases like fusarium (snow mould) getting a hold. If this happens, treat diseased patches without delay, using a good proprietary fungicide like those based on benomyl.

Those with large lawns could consider buying or hiring an electric lawn raker.

Rake up leaves as they fall in autumn. Otherwise they will blanket the lawn, smothering the grass to encourage disease and increase the worm population.

SPIKING AND TOPDRESSING

There are few lawns which don't benefit from spiking and topdressing in autumn or spring.

Working systematically over the lawn, spike down vertically with a garden fork, to a depth of about 15 cm (6 in). Spread soil based potting compost at the rate of about 1 kg per sq m (2 lbs per sq yd) with the back of a rake. And then lightly brush it into the spike holes. Be particularly thorough on any wet or over consolidated areas, such as the walkway onto the lawn, or where water is known to stand after heavy rain. Here it is best to brush in coarse sand after spiking, as opposed to potting compost, as it is on lawns overlying heavy soils. If there isn't time to treat the whole lawn, concentrate on compacted, tired looking areas. And for those who have neither the time nor the inclination to topdress, spiking alone is worthwhile; it improves aeration and relieves compaction. If not followed by topdressing, aim to spike more regularly – several times during the growing season.

DEALING WITH WORMS

Always brush off wormcasts (whips of soft mud) before mowing, otherwise they smear badly when moist, suffocating grasses and creating an uneven surface. Weeds and moss are quick to encroach. Where the worm population has reached an unacceptably high level, treat with a suitable worm killer in autumn or spring, but bear in mind that worms do a lot of good in aerating the soil. Only use chemical worm killers as a last resort.

WEED CONTROL

If left unchecked, weeds will eventually smother out the grasses. Don't worry about annual weeds like groundsel and shepherd's purse in new lawns, as they will soon be killed out by regular mowing. Don't worry about isolated persistent weeds either; they are simple to treat with a spot weeder, or to dig out by hand, infilling the holes with potting compost. Problems really begin where the likes of daisies, buttercups, plantain and dandelions are obviously taking over. In this situation, use a broad spectrum weedkiller, carefully following the maker's instructions. Some are complete, others need to be used in conjunction with fertilizer. The best time to apply weedkiller is when the grass is growing away freely in spring/early summer. It helps to rake the weeds into an upright position before application. Where the lawn is very weed infested, expect to give two applications, in successive years.

Application Apply weed and moss killers in mild, calm weather when the grass is dry and the soil moist. Don't apply during drought and don't apply to lawns under six months old. A weeder bar, fitted to a watering can, is useful for applying liquid chemicals.

The use of ground cover plants in shade makes a better alternative to grass.

MOSS CONTROL

Green moss in spring doesn't look too bad, but it browns badly as the season wears on. Modern chemical moss killers will eliminate it in the short term, but it will return unless something is done to improve the conditions which encouraged it to grow in the first place. Moss thrives on moist, poorly drained, starved soils which are inclined to be acidic. And in shaded areas it is likely to crowd out grasses very quickly. Too-close mowing and excessive rolling weaken grasses and encourage its growth, as does the regular use of mowers without rollers if the lawn is allowed to become puffy.

Adopt a routine of regular feeding, spiking and topdressing. And, in extreme cases, correct acidity (see page 85).

Most moss killers, including lawn sand, are applied between mid-spring and early summer. Read and follow instructions closely: some contain fertilizers, others weed killers and so on. About three weeks after application, the moss will be dead and ready to rake out. Any resulting bare patches should be reseeded (see page 81).

If treating moss in autumn, it is vital to choose a product suitable for the time of year, as many containing fertilizer promote vigorous disease-prone winter growth and are not to be recommended.

Note Never be tempted to rake out live moss – it's likely to spread further.

PROBLEM SOLVING

BUMPS AND HOLLOWS

Level out bumps and hollows to reduce scarring and scalping when mowing. Cut down through the uneven area of turf using a sharp spade and forming the letter 'H'. This makes it relatively easy to undercut and roll back the turf. Level out the undulations by removing soil, or adding topsoil or potting compost, as necessary. Firm, replace the turf and tamp down. Finally, fill in any cracks with potting compost.

Small hollows can be infilled gradually over a period of time, by spreading potting compost. But don't apply more than 12 mm (½ in) at any one time.

DAMAGED PATCHES

Cut out squares of blemished turf – these may be due to pollution or disease. Loosen up the soil beneath. Infill with potting compost, ensuring that, after firming, the surface is slightly above the surrounding lawn. This allows for settlement. Seed over in spring or autumn using 50 g of seed per sq m (1½ oz per sq yd), and then sift over with potting compost to cover. Protect from birds.

BARE AREAS

Spike, loosen up the surface with a rake, topdress with potting compost and seed over as above.

TREE ROOTS

Tree roots which have risen above the lawn surface are unsightly and can damage mower blades. Cover over with up to 5 cm (2 in) of good topsoil. Don't make it any deeper or you risk suffocation of tree roots. Grade the levels smoothly into the surrounding lawn before seeding over.

SHRUBS ENCROACHING ONTO THE LAWN

Neaten things up by recutting the lawn edges further back.

BROKEN EDGES

Where edges are broken, cut out damaged turf in squares, undercutting with a spade and making sure the turves are of even thickness throughout. Turn the turf completely round, lining up the good edge with the rest of the lawn. Tamp gently into place and infill behind with potting compost (Fig. 22). Top up in spring or autumn and oversow as for damaged patches.

Metal or polythene proprietary lawn strip fixed around lawn edges will prevent further damage. Set the top slightly below the lawn surface for ease of mowing.

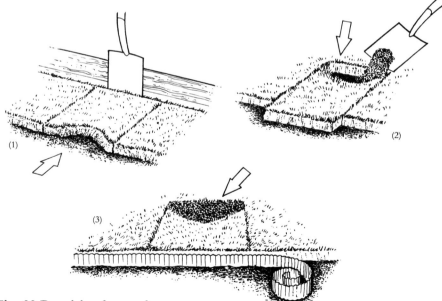

Fig. 22 Repairing lawn edges
1. Cut around damaged squares of turf – and then undercut.
2. Turn the turf round. And trim the edge to line up with the lawn edges on either side.
3. Infill the damaged area with potting compost in readiness for oversowing. And protect the new edge with proprietary edging strip.

CRACKING ON NEWLY SEEDED LAWNS – GAPS BETWEEN NEWLY LAID TURVES

Brush potting compost into the cracks or gaps. Spike, keep watered and topped up with more potting compost until the cracks and turves have knitted together. In extreme cases oversow in spring or autumn.

OVERSOWING A LAWN

Where the grass is thin, oversowing is feasible on both new and existing lawns. Wire rake, aiming to loosen the surface 12 mm (½ in) or so. Use a fork to ease up any compacted areas. Spread potting compost at the rate of 1–2 kg per sq m (2–4 lbs per sq yd), using the back of a solid tine rake. Oversow in autumn or spring with seed of a similar mixture to the existing lawn, allowing 50 g of seed per sq m (1½ oz per sq yd). Protect from birds and aim to keep watered.

SWINGS AND SLIDES

It is a good idea to construct a sand-filled pit beneath swings and around slide landings. This is to create a soft, safe landing and prevent puddling or over-compaction of the grass.

WALKWAYS ACROSS LAWNS

Sink in stepping slabs of some sort – slightly below the level of the lawn to avoid catching mower blades.

SPARSE GRASS UNDER THE SHADE OF TREES

Grass frequently dies out under spreading trees. This is usually due to the combined effects of summer dryness, winter drips and dense shade. In these situations, use low-growing, drought-resistant and shade-tolerant ground cover plants as an alternative to grass. Otherwise be prepared to replace the turf regularly. In the case of trees of tall upright habit, a collar of bare earth is much neater than sparse grass. Always leave a collar of bare earth when planting young trees or shrubs in grass; grass close in to their stems presents unacceptable competition for food and moisture.

GRASS UNDER THE SHADE OF WALLS AND BUILDINGS

Again shade-tolerant ground cover plants are a better choice than grass in these conditions.

GRAZED KNUCKLES

Lawns taken right up to a wall will inevitably lead to grazed knuckles when mowing. Consider putting down a paved strip between lawn and wall. Sink it slightly below the level of the lawn. Paving makes a labour-saving alternative to flower beds, which can be used to serve the same purpose. In the case of flower beds the soil must not be piled above the damp proof course.

CHAPTER 8

PROBLEM SOLVING

When dealing with pests and diseases, check on other factors which may have weakened plants and so made them more vulnerable to attack. Poor cultivations, the wrongful siting of plants, overcrowding – plus weather factors of wind, frost, sun and shade – can all contribute towards plant ill health. And old plants are particularly at risk.

Chemicals should not be used indiscriminately as an answer to all ills. This is on the grounds of pollution. And on the ground that the balance of nature is being upset as beneficial insects are being killed off along with the harmful. When chemicals are used, ensure the right one is bought for the job in hand. Some are insecticides – to deal with insect pests. Others are fungicides – to control fungal diseases. And some are mixtures — to deal with both pests and diseases. Rose sprays are often sold as mixtures.

Protect overwintering growing plants with plastic sheeting when winter washing dormant fruit trees.

Read the directions carefully. Mix and apply chemicals strictly according to the maker's recommendations. Delay spraying if children or pets are at play – or if pollinating insects are active. Store all chemicals, correctly labelled, well out of the reach of children and pets.

APHIDS
Aphids – greenfly and blackfly – will attack and weaken almost any garden plant. If they start to colonize around soft growing points – promptly remove the tips where it is practical to do so. These tips are often puckered and distorted. Then spray with an insecticide suited to the pest and the particular crop.

SLUGS
Slugs feed by night and hide during the day. They devour vast amounts of leaves, flowers, buds and stems. The best solution is to trap them with a proprietary slug bait. Alternatively, lay and weight down strips of black plastic on the soil surface. Slugs are attracted to the dark, moist security under the plastic. Lift the plastic daily and dispose of the slugs. Should natural methods of control fail, proprietary slug pellets and drenches are effective. Use them as the makers recommend. Don't allow rubbish to accumulate – and clear out hedge bottoms, as they make excellent breeding grounds.

EARWIGS
Earwigs are shiny, brown, night-feeding creatures with pincer-like tails. They do a lot of damage eating seedlings, leaves, buds, flowers and stems. Trap them in hayfilled, small, upturned pots – atop split canes. Push the canes into the soil amongst vulnerable plants. The earwigs will seek refuge in the hay during the day. Shake them out into a bucket of water where they can be destroyed.

CATERPILLARS
Caterpillars of one sort and another feed on buds, leaves, flowers, shoots and stems. In severe attacks the entire plant can be completely defoliated. Handpick these slow moving creatures in the early stages of an attack – paying particular attention to leaf undersides. If they get out of hand – spray with chemical. With food crops, ensure the requisite time lapse is left between spraying and harvesting.

BLACKSPOT AND MILDEW ON ROSES
Blackspot and mildew on roses are very common. With blackspot look for circular black spots on leaves and a likelihood of premature leaf dropping. Rose mildew manifests itself as a white powdery covering, mainly on buds and shoot tips. Spray at regular intervals throughout the growing season to combat these diseases. Dispose of fallen leaves and prunings promptly to prevent spread.

RED SPIDER MITES

Red spider mites may weaken climbers and wall plants in a hot dry summer. The leaves become hardened and speckled during an attack. Examine the undersides to reveal tiny mites and extensive very fine webbing. Spray with insecticide. Keep the plant moist by spraying overhead with clean water in the cool of the day.

SOIL PESTS

Soil pests like millipedes, cut worms and chafer grubs feed on the roots of plants. As do wireworms on newly cultivated grassland. The damaged, holed roots – with grubs perhaps embedded within – are most likely to be seen when harvesting root vegetables. But all soft, succulent rooted plants come under attack. Lettuce for instance may wither up and die as their roots are chewed. Trap these pests in pieces of potato or carrot tied onto split canes and buried near vulnerable crops under attack. Inspect the traps, dispose of the pests, and replenish the traps each day. Where problems persist, use soil insecticides.

BIRDS

To protect ripening fruits – as well as the bushes themselves, from bud stripping in winter – encase individual bushes in a netting cage, supported on a frame.

Keep birds off newly seeded grass – as well as other seeds – using dark wool and pegs. Push in the pegs, fairly close together, around the seeded area. Attach dark wool to the pegs about 10 cm (4 in) above the ground – criss-crossing the area in all directions. Use wool in preference to thread – it merely tips wings and feet to scare. Thread will cut to wound.

CHLOROSIS

Chlorosis is a condition in which leaves turn yellow and plants become unthrifty. It is most likely to occur where acid-loving plants like rhododendrons, azaleas, magnolias, camellias, some heathers and to a lesser extent roses – are grown in lime rich soils. Treat ailing plants with sequestered iron.

PLANT PROTECTION AGAINST THE WEATHER

It is young plants that are most likely to need protection from the weather.
Wind protection In exposed gardens, protect newly set out plants – individually – with fine mesh netting attached to a light framework.
Sun protection Shade young plants from direct midday sun during the first season after planting. Fine mesh netting is useful for the purpose.
Frost protection Give the roots of frost-sensitive young plants extra protection by putting down a minimum 5 cm (2 in) layer of straw or bark in autumn. Keep it in place with pegged down netting and leave undisturbed until spring. Shrubs like camellias and magnolias have frost sensitive roots when young – but are hardy when established.

RELIABLE GARDEN PLANTS FOR OUTDOORS

ORNAMENTAL TREES

Cotoneaster 'Hybridus Pendulus'
Crataegus prunifolia (thorn)
Ilex × altaclarensis 'Camelliifolia' (holly)
Laburnum × waterii 'Vossii'
Magnolia × soulangiana
Malus sargentii (flowering crab)
Prunus cerasifera 'Nigra' (flowering plum)
Prunus 'Kanzan' (flowering cherry)
Sorbus aucuparia (mountain ash)
Syringa 'Charles Joly' (lilac)

FLOWERING SHRUBS

Berberis darwinii
Buddleia davidii 'Nanho Purple'
Forsythia 'Lynwood'
Hydrangea macrophylla 'Blue Wave'
Hypericum calcinum
Mahonia aquifolium
Potentilla arbuscula
Spiraea 'Gold Flame'
Viburnum tinus
Weigela 'Bristol Ruby'

CLIMBERS AND WALL SHRUBS

Chaenomeles 'Knap Hill Scarlet'
  (flowering quince)
Chimonanthus 'Grandiflorus'
  (winter sweet)
Clematis 'Nelly Moser'
Cotoneaster horizontalis
Garrya elliptica
Hedera helix 'Goldheart' (ivy)
Jasminum nudiflorum (winter jasmine)
Parthenocissus henryana (virginia creeper)
Pyracantha angustifolia (firethorn)
Wisteria sinensis

DWARF AND SLOW-GROWING CONIFERS

Chamaecyparis lawsoniana 'Ellwoods Gold'
C. pisifera 'Boulevard'
Juniperus communis 'Compressa'
J. c. 'Hibernica'
J. c. 'Depressa Aurea'
J. × media 'Old Gold'
Picea glauca albertiana 'Conica'
Pinus mugo 'Mops'
Thuja occidentalis 'Rheingold'
T. orientalis 'Aurea Nana'

HEDGING PLANTS

Berberis
Buxus (box)
Carpinus (hornbeam)
× *Cupressocyparis* (Leyland cypress)
Fagus (beech)

Ligustrum (privet)
Prunus
Taxus (yew)
Thuja
Viburnum tinus

HERBACEOUS BORDER PERENNIALS

Anemone japonica (Japanese anemone)
Aster 'Novii Belgii' (Michaelmas daisy)
Dianthus (border pinks & carnations)
Helenium
Hemerocallis (day lily)
Hosta

Kniphofia (red hot poker)
Liatris (blazing star)
Paeonia
Phlox – (border perennial)
Sedum spectabile
Solidago (golden rod)

EASY ROCK PLANTS

Alyssum (*aurinia*)
Armeria (thrift)
Aubrieta

Campanula (bell flower)
Dianthus (rock pinks)
Helianthemum (rock rose)

Phlox
Saxifraga
Thymus (thyme)

HARDY BULBS

Anemone
Crocus
Narcissi (daffodil)

Hyacinthus
Lilium
Muscari (grape hyacinth)

Scilla
Galanthus (snowdrop)
Tulipa

SUMMER BEDDING PLANTS

Ageratum
Alyssum (*Lobularia*)
Aster (*Callistephus*)
Begonia

Geranium (*Pelargonium*)
Impatiens (busy lizzie)
Lobelia
Marigold – French (*Tagetes*)

Pansy (viola)
Petunia
Salvia
Verbena

SPRING BEDDING PLANTS

Bellis (double daisy)
Myosotis (forget–me–not)
Pansy (viola)

Polyanthus
Primrose
Cheiranthus (wallflower)

INDEX

Acidity, 15–26
Alpines, 17
Aphids, 92
Apple, 76–77
Aspect, 15
Aucuba, 17
Azalea, 32, 35, 36, 73

Bedding plants, 58, 60
Birds, protection from, 93
Blackberry, 78
Blackcurrant, 32, 77–78
Blackspot, 92
Brassicas, 65
Broad bean, 44
Brussels Sprout, 65
Bulbs, 50–51, 60
Busy lizzie, 45

Cabbage, 65
Calceolaria, 45
Camellia, 15–16, 32, 35
Caterpillars, 92
Cauliflower, 65
Chemical soil conditioners, 31
Cherry, 77
Chlorosis, 93
Clematis, 32
Climate, 14, 16
Climbers, 56–57
Compost, 25, 30, 32, 38–40
Conifers, 32, 67, 75–76
Containers, plants grown in, 35, 37, 61, 63
Corms, division, 50–51
Cotoneaster, 17
Crazy paving, 12
Crocus, 50–51, 60
Cultivation, 22–28
Currants, 46, 77–78
Cuttings, 44–48

Daffodil, 50–51, 60
Dahlia, 32
Deadheading, 74
Delphinium, 32
Designing gardens, 10–17
Digging, 22–24
Division, 49–51
Double digging, 24
Drainage, 19–22
Drill sowing, 42–44
Drought, 23

Earthing up, 27
Earwigs, 92
Escallonia, 46

Euonymus, 17
Evergreen plants, 17

F_1 and F_2 hybrids, 41
Fencing, 8–9, 13–14, 85
Fertility, 29–40
Fetilizer, 33, 34–36
Footpaths, 8
Forget-me-not, 44
Forking, 24–25
Forsythia, 46, 72
Foxglove, 44
Frames, 10
Frost protection, 93
Fruit, 10, 17, 37, 63–64
    pruning and training, 76–78
Geranium , 45, 46
Gooseberry, 46, 78
Grass clippings, 33, 39, 84
Gravel paths, 12
Greenhouses, 10
Ground cover, 20

Heading back, 68
Heathers, 32, 36
    peg layering, 51
Hedges, 9, 14
    planting, 56, 61
    pruning and clipping, 67, 68, 74–76
Heliotrope, 45
Herbs, 17
Hoeing, 25–27
Hydrangea
    climbing, 56
    evergreen, 48

Ivy, 56

Laurel, 48
Lawns, 79–90
    aerating, 25, 28, 86
    drainage, 21
    edging, 84–85
    feeding, 85
    levelling, 18–19
    mowing, 82–85
    rolling, 85
    scarifying, 85–86
    topdressing, 86
    trees, 89, 90
    turfing, 79, 80–81
    weeds and moss, 86–88
Layering, 51
Leafmold, 30, 32, 40
Leek, 65
Lettuce, 65

Levelling, 18–19
Lilies, 32
Liming, 35–36, 85
Loganberry, 78
Lopping, 68–69

Manure, 23, 29–32
    green manuring, 31–32
Marrow, 44, 65
Mexican orange, 48
Mildew, 92
Minerals, 31
Mulching, 32–33, 36
    with polythene, 33

Narcissus, 50–51, 60
Nuisance, 9

Onion, 65

Parsnip, 44
Paths, 12
Patios, 10
Pear, 77
Peat, 32
Periwinkle, 20
Pests, 23, 91–93
Pieris, 32
Pinching, 68
Pit planting, 53–56
Planting season, 52
Plum, 77
Potato, 36, 64
Potentilla, 17
Propagation, 41–51
Pruning, 66–78
Pyracantha, 72

Raking, 27–28, 85–86
Raspberry, 63–64, 77
Red spider mite, 93
Redcurrant, 78
Reverted shoots, 72
Rhododendron, 15–16, 32, 35, 36, 61, 73
Rock gardens, 17, 26, 57
Rose of sharon, 20
Roses, 57, 92
    pruning, 73–74
Runner bean, 64

Safety hazards, 8–9
Seedlings, 37
Seeds, 41–44
    F_1 and F_2 hybrids, 41
    sowing, 42–44
    storing, 41–42
Shade, 16, 17, 90, 93

Shallot, 65
Shelter, 15
Shrubs, 53–56
    pruning, 66–67, 71–73
Slugs, 92
Snowdrop, 51
Soil, 15–16
    acidity, 35–36
    aerating, 23, 86
    clay, 16, 23, 29
    cultivation, 22–28
    depth, 52
    drainage, 19–22
    fertility, 29–40
    management, 16
    pests, 93
    pH measurement, 16
    sandy, 16, 23, 29
    texture, 16, 29–40, 36
    topsoil, 15
Stem cuttings, 44·48
Stepping stones, 12
Stopping, 68
Strawberrry, 49–50, 64
Suckers, 72–72
Sump, construction of, 21–22
Sun, protection from, 93
Sweet pea, 44

Tomato, 65
Tools, 8, 22, 29, 41, 52, 69–70, 79
Town gardens, 17
Trees, 63, 76–77
    on lawns, 89, 90
    planting, 53–56
    pruning, 66–67, 71, 76–77
    safety aspect, 9
Tulip, 60

Vegetables, 10, 17, 35, 37
    earthing up, 27
    planting, 64·65
    soil cultivation, 22
Virginia creeper, 56

Wall plants, 56·57
Walls, 8–9, 13
Water gardens, 17
Watering, 36–38, 85
Weeds, 23, 24, 25, 39, 86–87
Weigela, 46
Whitecurrant, 78
Wind, 17, 93
Wisteria, 32
Worms, 86